10/16/2000

Dave

Happy Selling!

How to Become a Millionaire Selling Remodeling

I did it—and so can you!

Phil Rea

Five Star Publications, Incorporated
Chandler, Arizona U.S.A.

Published 1998 by Five Star Publications, Incorporated
Chandler, Arizona
Printed in the United States of America

Five Star Publications, Incorporated
P.O. Box 6698
Chandler, AZ 85246-6698

Library of Congress Cataloging-in-Publication Data

Rea, Phil. 1953–
How to become a millionaire selling remodeling
I did it—and so can you! / Phil Rea.
p. cm.
ISBN 1–877749–29–X
1. Advertising. 2. Dwellings--Remodeling--Economic aspects.
I. Title.
HF6161.R3R4 1998
690'.24--dc21 97-46827
CIP

Publishing Consultant: Linda F. Radke
Editor: Paul M. Howey
Cover Design: Lynlie J. Hermann
Jacket Photography: John Warters
Proofreader: Sal Caputo
Typesetting Layout: Cyndi Keene

Acknowledgements

Without the following people, and a number that I will certainly fail to mention, this book would have been something that I merely thought about, but would likely never have accomplished.

My grandmother, DoDo, who encouraged me to search for the good in every person.

My deceased mother and father, Dorothy Jane and Jim, who left me with memories of "you can." They were my first and best sales managers.

My wife and best friend, Bennie, whose encouragement, advice, and listening ear have taken me further than I ever thought about going.

My children, Amanda, Ryan, and Elizabeth, who taught me "hotshot" salesman away from home only means you have to be "hotshot" daddy at home.

My friend and sales partner, Ron Buhl, who had the nerve to put into practice what I told him to do. He taught me how to teach others.

To the many of you who have become known to me, not as remodeling salespeople or contractors, but as true friends. Thank you for your support and inspiration.

To almighty God, who allows me to be.

Phil Rea

Chapter # Table of Contents

Chapter

Foreword

For the twenty years I've worked in the remodeling industry, I never met anybody who's made a million dollars — except Phil Rea.

Phil has all the qualities of a successful salesman. He genuinely likes people. He cares about them. He's curious. He asks good questions, and he really listens to the answers. He can listen to all the reasons a remodeling prospect doesn't want to buy, like "the price is too high" or "remodeling is too disruptive right now" and demonstrate his understanding and concern for that prospect's reluctance.

Then, his competitive spirit takes over — his desire to win, to close, to succeed, to show that prospect he can make them a satisfied customer. That's when he earns his living. By gently, but firmly, overcoming objections until the prospect is comfortable, trusting, ready to buy...sold!

Most remodeling contractors make an art of construction. They call themselves craftsmen because they create beautiful spaces. But these craftsmen don't get all the opportunity they should to create spaces. They can't build it until they sell it. So, in remodeling, selling comes first!

No one understands this better than Phil Rea. By learning and applying this art of selling in his remodeling business, Phil stands out in an industry that's overcrowded with remodelers who want to make money, but don't.

If you are one of these remodelers, I urge you to read this book. You may not want to do everything Phil suggests because it's not your style. But make selling a priority. Make it fun. Try a Phil Rea approach that does fit your style. You'll be surprised at how receptive your prospects are to being sold.

Who knows, you might even earn a million dollars. Nothing brings success better than being successful.

Peter H. Miller
Founding Publisher, Remodeling Magazine
Co-founder, *Remodelers* Show

Introduction

Driving home from my job as a car salesman one Saturday afternoon in December 1979, I was listening to a financial expert on the radio talking about where the millionaires of the next decade were going to come from. I found what he had to say so interesting that I sat in my driveway clinging to his every word. He said the new millionaires were going to come from service-oriented businesses, such as those in cleaning, lawn care, and home remodeling.

A few days later, a friend of mine, who was a former car salesman, entered my office grinning proudly as he showed me how much he had earned the previous month by selling remodeling. I was impressed. Familiar with his abilities, I knew I could do at least as well as he had done. Later that evening, I talked with my wife about the advantages of being in the car business versus the remodeling business. A decision was made and I reported to work the following Monday morning to begin what turned out to be a fabulously rewarding career selling remodeling.

The guy on the radio was right about at least one person becoming a millionaire in the service business. Was I the first one? Of course not. Was I the only one? Certainly not. Am I going to be the last one? Let's hope not! Remodeling is a business in which you can obtain substantial wealth. It didn't take me very long — roughly fifteen years. At the age of forty-one, I was able to retire from the business!

In this book, I'm not going to teach you how to become a remodeler. Most of you are already good at your craft. Rather, I'll share what few of you do know: how to *make money* at your craft. I urge you to start investing more effort in the little things that you don't think will make any difference in your success formula. Sit down and talk with me for thirty minutes and then talk with the average remodeling salesperson for thirty minutes. Chances are, you will notice very little difference between us.

What makes my income ten times what his might be? It's in those little, day-to-day things such as calling a prospect back within the hour, being on time for appointments, sending a customer a get-well card, etc. Sam Walton (the founder of Wal-Mart and, prior to his death, the richest man in America) had the philosophy that it was easier to change a thousand things by one percent than it was to change one thing by a thousand percent.

The amount of time, money, and effort that went into the spaceship Challenger could not keep it from blowing up. It was a single o-ring that caused the Challenger to explode in flight. Little things are often the difference between success and failure.

It is my sincere desire that this book will assist you on your path to success.

Chapter 1

IS THERE ANY MONEY IN THE REMODELING BUSINESS?

Years ago, one of my best friends and I thought we'd hit the big time as car salesmen, and so we joined a country club where we could play our one round of golf a week. One particular afternoon as we were taking our clubs out of the trunk, a gentleman pulled up next to us in a big new Lincoln Continental with out-of-state tags. As we were getting ready to tee off on the first hole, the man asked if he could join us, and we said sure.

Over the next few holes, I qualified the heck out of him. I couldn't help myself. It's just part of who I am. Whether I'm trying to acquire information to make a sale or just out on the golf course, I'm firing the questions. "What kind of work do you do?" "Optometrist" was his response. "Do you have your own business?" "Yes, I own several laboratories where the glasses are made." "Are any of those labs in this area?" "No, I own a second home in Kingsmill and spend several months a year there." (Kingsmill is one of the most upscale communities in our area. I couldn't have afforded my primary home there, much less a second one.)

A few minutes later, out of the blue, my friend says, "Doc, let me ask you a question. Is there any money in the eyeglass business?" I thought I was going to fall out of the golf cart. I whispered to him, "Man, are you crazy? Weren't you listening to anything he said? Of course, there has got to be money in the eyeglass business." My friend wasn't one to take anything for granted. Just because the man showed money didn't mean he'd made it from his eyeglass business. For all my friend knew, the man's wife may have inherited the money. He didn't ask a bunch of questions and make assumptions based on the answers as I was doing. He was like "Dragnet's" Joe Friday, "Just the facts, sir."

Many of you are wondering if there is any money in the remodeling business. The answer is a resounding "yes!" The real question is, "Can you see it?" Linda Case, in her book *Making & Managing Money*, said, "Few remodelers get wealthy from their remodeling businesses. Some get wealthy by investing the money generated by remodeling in land, buildings, and other businesses." When I read that statement, the same thought occurred to me that does when I speak with many remodelers who are struggling to make a living: It just doesn't have to be that way.

I wish you could have heard that message from the 1979 radio broadcast about all the millionaires who would come out of the remodeling industry. When it comes to making money, it helps to be in an industry in which money is being spent. It's projected that over $125 billion is spent in remodeling each year. My dad used to say about me that, if I could find someone with $10, I could talk them out of half of it. Even if he were exaggerating, I know I can get my share of that $125 billion. If that number doesn't do anything for you, think about this: *There will soon be more money spent on remodeling homes than on constructing new ones*. That's pretty impressive when you consider the average remodeling project is around $5,000 and the average new home is around $135,000.

If you are still concerned about the security and opportunity for financial reward in this industry, just get in your car and start riding through neighborhoods. Spend one hour writing down what you see that needs to be done to these homes. That little exercise has always given me a great sense of security.

I don't know what else I can say to convince you that you are in a big-money business. You cannot blame the industry if you are not getting your share (that's another issue that we will address). The old 20/80 rule still applies: 20 percent of the people make 80 percent of the money. That doesn't mean you can't be in the 20 percent arena. Perhaps you're afraid to make money! You think you are stealing instead of selling.

It is often hard for the person who manufactures a product and knows what it costs to make it to then turn around and sell it at retail. In many cases, that is what remodeling salespeople have to do. I liken it to the automobile assembly-line operators who know what it costs to build a car. If those same operators go to work as salespeople on a retail car lot, many would have a hard time selling that car for two times what it cost in labor and materials to produce.

An old-time remodeler told me that many years ago the United States Government had consultants it sent out to help small businesses establish the percent of profit they needed in order to prosper in their particular industry. The consultant who worked with him said that, with all the overhead and unknowns that are associated with remodeling, you need to total your labor and material and triple that number. I wish I'd heard that when I first started. You see, when we don't know any different, we can sell the product for whatever we are told to sell it for.

The primary reason there is big money to be made in this business is because you set the price. There is no such thing as comparing apples to apples unless the prospect is presented the exact same product being installed by the exact same installer.

My job as a salesperson is to be firmly convinced of the value of my product and then convince my potential customer of that worth. I sold a job to a successful businessman who had already received a price from a competitor. He told me he'd been given a price that was $2,500 less than mine (that represented a 15 percent difference). I asked him what product they were using and he told me. My reply was, "I'm not going to mislead you. While the product I'm recommending is a more expensive product than what they have recommended, it's not $2,500 more product. What I can tell you is that I have siding mechanics I could send to do your house that would cost you less money, but I'm sending you the best I have, and they're worth the $2,500." My prospect said, "Write it up." We talked about something that could not be compared: the person actually doing the work.

When you go to the grocery store and shop, there are a number of ways to compare value — several products from which to choose, the number of ounces versus the price per ounce, and maybe you have a coupon to use. You have products side by side.

In the remodeling business, we manufacture many of our products. There is no product to compare to until it's produced. The only way to get a true comparison is to have two companies produce the same product on the same house for the same customer. I've never met a prospect willing to pay for that.

I have a friend who owns a furniture store. Let me share with you a little information about the pricing formula used in his business. Let's say the product on the floor is $1,000. If my friend is having trouble moving the product, he puts it on sale for 50 percent off. At that point, he will still have a profit margin of 33 percent. In other words, that $1000 piece cost them $333. He is operating on a mark-up of 300 percent — exactly what the government consultant told the remodeler to mark up.

I'm not telling you to mark up 300 percent. As a matter of fact, I'm not going to tell you how much to mark up. That has to be your call. You're the one who has to be sold so that you can sell others. However, I do want you to think for a moment how much more liability you might have than the furniture dealer. What's the worst that can happen to the furniture dealer if someone doesn't like the piece of furniture? They take it back and try to sell it again or, if there is a defect, they have to send it back to the factory or sell it as damaged goods. None of these scenarios is all that bad.

What's the worst that can happen to you as a remodeler when a customer does not like your product? You have to take it back. In most cases, that means tearing it down and starting over again. Rarely do you have a product you can take back or resell. Most often, it means buying more materials and additional labor at your expense. Unless the customer has paid you in advance (joke), you have little choice but to satisfy them and move on to a job where you can hope to make money. As a remodeling salesperson, you have much at stake. There's a lot of liability hanging out there. That's the negative side. The positive side is that you set your own prices and that means you can give yourself a raise anytime you want one, whether you deserve one or not. You're in a position to make as much money as the best doctors and lawyers. As with them, the customer finds out your worth after you have delivered your product. And, if your product is as good as you say it is, "Good golly, Miss Molly, the money will roll in."

Don't let anyone tell you otherwise, there is big money to be made in the remodeling business. Now that doesn't automatically entitle you to it. The question is, can you see yourself making your share of it? If not, are you proud that you work from sunrise to sunset for a meager wage? That you can't take off to attend a baseball game, much less consider a family vacation?

Money is a relative term. One person's ceiling is another person's floor. There is enough money to be made in this business to satisfy anybody's ceiling. You only have to establish what that ceiling is for you. Can you imagine having a job where you worked all day and, at five o'clock, you went in to your boss and he said to you, "There's plenty of money in that safe. Go in and get whatever you feel you deserve." Well, ladies and gentlemen, those of us who are remodeling salespeople have exactly that kind of job. We make what we deserve.

Some of you would make much more money if someone other than you determined what you deserved. To those of you who cannot make the mental transition from that of wage earner to wealthy entrepreneur, please — for your sake as well as your loved ones, — find a good, salaried job working for someone else. For those of you who have a real desire to make some serious money, hold on.

It will be a roller-coaster ride filled with lots of actions, thrills, and excitement. But, when it's all over, you will be glad you chose the roller coaster instead of the security of the merry-go-round.

Chapter 2

MAKE MONEY THE WAY YOU KNOW HOW

Late one Saturday afternoon, I received a call from one of my brothers. He is best described as an investment entrepreneur who makes his living looking for deals. He called me to inform me he had come across an opportunity that only comes around, if you're lucky, once a year. He'd become aware of a company that had lost 66 percent of its value the day before. Its stock had been trading at $36 and, in one day, fell to $12. His findings revealed that a key employee had gone bad and the market greatly overreacted. When the market opened on Monday, he said the stock should have what he called a "dead chicken bounce." This was new terminology to me. He explained that a dead chicken will bounce some when it hits the floor. This stock was going to do the same thing, he said, and the key is to be positioned to capitalize on that bounce. "You're going to owe me for this one," he added. "Send me my commission check."

The next day, Sunday, I hurt my back so badly I was unable to walk and was confined to bed rest on Monday. I did, however, find the energy to place an order for the largest single volume of stock I had ever purchased. I bragged to my wife how much money I was going to make just lying on my back. My brother had me so sold I was even talking like him. On Monday, the stock dropped another dollar. My brother called me and said, "We're right where we want to be, the bleeding has stopped. The stock didn't take another big hit today." Somewhat unnerved, I asked, "What happened to that 'dead chicken bounce'?" "Don't worry," he said "it's coming." By the end of that week — the week when I was supposedly participating in an opportunity that only comes around *maybe* once a year — I had lost $16,200. I was now scared about losing my entire investment, so I took the loss and sold out. Why? I was in an arena that was foreign to me. I knew absolutely nothing firsthand about this company. I knew only what my brother had told me and what he knew, somebody had told him. I couldn't be mad at him since he thought he was doing his little brother a good deed. Besides, he had invested more than twice the money I had. He had two bruises, one to his checkbook and the other to his ego. Did I have to sell? No, I had options. I could have purchased more stock in an effort to reduce my average cost per share. That, however, would have taken more nerve than I could muster. Or I could have held out longer than a week to see if the stock would turn around.

Have you ever had anything like that happen to you? If you don't have it to lose, it won't happen. But, just as sure as you start making money, more opportunities will come your way than you ever imagined. Many of them will appear to be "no way to lose on this opportunity" type of deals. Until my brother called, I had managed to avoid them myself. I took my eye off the ways that I knew to make money. I was depending on someone else to make me money in a product I knew nothing about.

As a remodeler, I don't recall ever losing money on a job. I had done several thousand jobs and never lost a dime. Of course, I had some jobs that did not produce profit and, had I factored in the cost of missed opportunities, I lost money. But no job ever cost me more to produce in labor and material than what I had sold it for.

One of the reasons I was able to be so profitable was that I steadfastly refused to get sidetracked. Every few months, someone would call our company and ask if we would build a new house for them. I wasn't the least bit interested. I was aware of the margins in new construction and knew they were not what I was accustomed to. I was also aware that remodeling projects and new home construction are two different things.

While I had seen builders jump in and out of the remodeling business, rarely had I seen a remodeler go into building homes on a full-time basis. On the other hand, I had seen many builders go bankrupt. I knew a lot of remodelers who didn't pay their bills on time, but seldom did one go bankrupt.

So what's the harm in building a new house once in awhile? As easy as it looked, something didn't appear right about it. I was making more money than I had ever imagined in remodeling and I wasn't willing to risk it by doing something else. I sold more than one job by telling prospects that we were strictly a remodeling company and then educating them on the difference between a remodeling carpenter and a new construction carpenter. I never left without telling them it was very important to inquire if the other companies they were talking with did any new construction. I advised them that, if they did hire one of those companies, to insist that they put only their remodeling carpenters on their project. This often created enough doubt in the prospects' minds that they hired us. With us, they were assured of getting remodeling carpenters.

If there is more money to be made doing new houses, build new houses. If you think the money is in remodeling, then do remodeling. Don't ever let "good" rob you of the "best."

Other businesses (for example, rental property, or handyman specials that can be fixed up and sold at good profit margins) do appear to be compatible with the remodeling business. It might appear that a good fixer-upper would be nice to have around to use as a filler to keep the crews busy during slack periods. What could possibly be wrong with that?

A rule of business I particularly like is: *Never put yourself in a position to be a competitor to the customer you are serving*. For example, you badly need your electrician to be in two places — your customer's house and your own fixer house. If you don't put yourself in a position to make those decisions, you won't be faced with that conflict. I challenge those of you who have been in business for some time and tried a little of everything, like building a new house and fixing up an old one, to go back and see where you have made your money. I'm confident you will find it's from working for your customers one at a time. Having rental property to which you're enslaved is not the best position to be in. You may not be able to sell them because of capital gains taxes or, when you're packing up to go to the beach, you get a call that someone's water heater has gone out. In building new homes, you could end up with a house that sits for months. Even if it's a pre-sold house, it's highly unlikely that your return will be anywhere near the return you routinely earn on your remodeling projects.

I love remodeling! You don't have to spend a dime until you have a contract. I started my company with $1,000. My first job was a $25,000 sale with a $15,000 deposit. That customer got me off and running. How many businesses have that potential? None of which I'm aware. So stop looking around for other ways to make money. You're already in the right place.

A source of frustration for me has always been salespeople who are involved in selling other products on a part-time basis, such as the real-estate person who is selling a multilevel marketing plan on the side. What salesperson ever goes home at the end of a day where one more phone call or visit to a previous or prospective client could not have been made? The salesperson's job is never finished. We just stop periodically for rest, relaxation, and to take care of those other areas in our lives that need nurturing.

Tell me how a person who is involved in direct sales (I'm not talking about someone who is in retail sales and works a scheduled forty-hour week) can stop selling one product and start selling another. One of those selling jobs is not getting all the effort it deserves. I can tell you right now, no salesperson would be working in my organization who is selling any product other than mine. I see it as a blatant conflict of interest. It's just that simple. I want every hour that salesperson has to sell to be spent selling my goods and services. There is absolutely nothing wrong with someone selling products part-time. Many people have done extremely well doing just that. I am, however, saying there is something wrong with a commissioned salesperson investing energy to sell someone else's products. Get on one horse, whatever that horse may be, and ride it as hard as you can. When you get tired of that horse or it gets tired of you, get on another one and ride it just as hard — but ride only one at a time. A truly professional salesperson doesn't need more than one horse.

You can rest assured that, when you do start making money, you will have a new set of concerns. One will be how to handle all those investment opportunities that will be introduced to you. Let me tell you about my two all-time favorites. One night, a guy called me at my house and asked me to go in with him to buy an airplane. I told him, "I'm not a pilot, never have been, and don't have any interest in becoming one." He said, "Well, I thought you might be interested in the investment opportunity." "How much is this plane?" I asked. To which he responded, "$1,500." I told him, "Man, I wouldn't even buy a used car that didn't cost more than $1,500, much less buy an airplane!"

Another time, a guy came to my office and informed me that he was going to try out for the Senior PGA Tour. He thought it would take him about a year or two before he could expect enough winnings to support himself. He asked me to invest $25,000 in his golfing future. I'll admit, this guy was a good amateur golfer, but he'd never even won any of the amateur events he'd entered. This was a man in a classic mid-life crisis. I didn't want to hurt his feelings. So, I didn't say, "No. Do you think I'm totally stupid?" Instead, I asked, "How in the world could I justify going home this evening and telling my wife I had given somebody $25,000 to play golf?" His response was, "You don't have to tell her." I thought about that guy many times after that. Had he taken the nerve it took to ask me for the $25,000 to go play golf and applied that same nerve to his business, he never would have been in my office.

Make money the way you know how, and let others make money the way they know how.

Chapter 3

YOUR PRIORITIES SHOULD BE YOUR PRIORITIES

With only a few days remaining in his second month in the remodeling business, a young salesperson and I sat down to have lunch. I asked him how things were going. He told me he had sold $75,000 worth of business in his first month and had been greatly encouraged. I, too, thought this was good since he had set $600,000 as his goal for his first year. "Where do you stand for this month?" I asked. "This has really been a hard-luck month for me," he answered. "I have written another $75,000 worth of business, but it's all been either non-financeable or the folks have canceled." I asked him to tell me about each of the jobs.

He described one particular job that he had spent a great deal of time selling. He had done several sets of drawings because the customers owned two houses and they couldn't decide which one they wanted to remodel. It was even more difficult because he had to compete with another remodeling company. Although getting the deal financed had been somewhat of a challenge, he had managed to get it approved. The only thing keeping the job from being totally wrapped up was that the husband had some concerns over the interest rate.

"Well, it sounds like you at least can salvage that job," I offered. "It won't happen this month," he sighed. When I asked him why not, he told me, "I have so many other appointments that it will be the middle of next week before I can get back with them."

It was all I could do to respond in a manner that appeared even half-way civil. How could a commissioned salesperson who had made absolutely no money for the entire month even consider going on a new appointment when he was perhaps just minutes from getting a paycheck on an existing one? The priorities that this salesperson and I placed on money were obviously quite different. Unfortunately, this was not unique. Too many fail to recognize that their priority as salespeople is just that — to *sell*.

I recently read in the newspaper that a friend of mine was the salesperson of the month at the auto dealer where I do business. Shortly after that, I took my car in for service and congratulated him on the award. I asked how things were going this month. "I've got out one-half a unit," was his answer. (One-half a unit is car lingo that means he had split the commission on the sale of just one car.) I immediately felt bad that I was consuming any of his precious time. He had a family to support and he needed to be selling. He didn't need to be talking with me, he needed to be waiting on customers who came on the lot or, if that weren't the case, he needed to get in his car and go door to door if necessary.

Napoleon Hill once did an interview with Thomas Alva Edison. Edison, who had conducted over 10,000 experiments before producing the light bulb, told Hill, "If I did not already accomplish what I set out to accomplish, I wouldn't be having this interview. I would be in the lab working on the bulb." Edison clearly had his priorities.

All of us are capable of having bad months, but a remodeling salesperson who sells ten jobs one month can't sit down and sell nothing the next month. A car salesperson who sells sixteen cars one month, can't get by selling one-half a car the next month. Some months, we easily meet the quotas we set for ourselves. Other months, it is much more difficult. The bottom line, however, is that we need to make it our vocational priority to obtain our goals each and every month.

As salespeople, you should go home at the end of each day and ask yourselves, "Did I sell something today? If not, what did I do today that put me closer to a sale tomorrow?" If you don't like your answers, you'd better hit the ground running tomorrow.

Chapter 4

DON'T BE TOO BUSY SELLING TO SELL THE JOB!

I was hired as a consultant for a remodeling company and went out on several sales calls with four of their salespeople. It was amazing to see how differently they handled their appointments. What it boiled down to was that two of them made sure they allowed enough time to sell, while the other two didn't.

The reason that two of them didn't have time to sell was that they had scheduled more appointments than they could effectively handle. Notice I used the words *effectively handle*. There is a big difference in effectively handling a sales call versus merely showing up for the appointment. Of course, how many appointments you can effectively handle varies according to the type of jobs you sell. For example, design-build salespeople probably have their hands full working just two leads a week. On the other hand, those who sell such specialty items as windows, siding, roofing, etc., can easily handle two to four appointments a day.

Some of you are probably saying, "I go on as many as six or seven appointments a day." I believe you. That's exactly what my "too busy to sell" sales reps were doing. They'd go on one appointment while already planning how to get to the next appointment on time instead of doing whatever was necessary to sell this one they were on. These "too busy to sell" folks were already worn out by Wednesday. They arrived at their appointments out of breath and they left panting. They gave the distinct impression that they didn't even want to be there.

The prospects didn't know and, quite frankly, didn't care what was going on in the salespersons' lives. They did know what *wasn't* happening. They were not being given full attention and service by the sales rep that they deserved. As a matter of fact, neither one of my "too busy to sell" salespeople even introduced themselves, much less me.

One of the prospects asked the salesperson for the measurement of a step three times. He told her what he thought it was the first time. The reason she asked him two more times was she wanted to *see* it measured. The height of that step was critical to the design of the project being discussed. Was he right about the height of the step? Probably. But people are visual in nature and, as a result, effective selling is showing and not telling. My "too busy to sell" salesperson's tape measure was in the car, and going out to get it would slow him down. Actually, it probably would have taken only a couple of minutes, but those were minutes he didn't feel he could invest. After spending just fifteen minutes with the prospect, the sales rep did ask her when she was going to be making a decision. She said, "I have another company coming to give me an estimate." That was just what he wanted to hear in order to rationalize his own sales inadequacy. In his mind, her statement vindicated him and his poor effort to sell her because she was obviously just shopping.

My second "too busy to sell" salesperson was standing out in the yard talking with the husband when the wife drove up. "Too busy" didn't even acknowledge her and the husband couldn't have introduced him because "too busy to sell" had not even introduced himself! A skilled salesperson knows that products don't sell, people do. You don't have to invite the prospects over to Friday night dinner, but engaging them in conversation is required.

More than once I've had a prospect call me and cancel an appointment because they had already bought from someone else. I'm certain they encountered the type of salesperson who was "not too busy to sell." That's the type of salespeople my second two from this company were. Instead of seeing how quickly they could get out of there, they spent nearly two hours on each appointment.

My first "not too busy to sell" salesperson was a kitchen designer. I asked her what her goal was for the appointment prior to our arrival. Knowing she wasn't going to design and contract the job right then, she said her goal was to convince the prospect that her company was the best one for her project. Both she and my other "not to busy to sell" salesperson spent the majority of their time doing just that. The kitchen designer even found out what brought the prospect to the area, how many children she had, how old the daughter was, how at her age she felt about coming to the area and what her interests were. When she found out her daughter was a competitive swimmer, "not to busy to sell" went as far as to tell her about some swimming clubs in the neighborhood. She was aware of the importance of relationship selling. She realized that while anyone can sell a kitchen, not everyone takes the time to find out the real important issues such as "how your teenage daughter feels" about being uprooted and how you are dealing with that.

Both of my "not too busy to sell" salespeople went through a company presentation book and talked about the background of the company, shared some of their successes, and showed pictures of completed projects. I wish you had been there to see for yourself how engrossed the prospects got and the expressions on their faces as they viewed certain projects. If you had, I know you wouldn't go on another appointment without your presentation book.

Have I told you anything you don't already know? Probably not. Can you imagine ever conducting yourself as my first two salespeople did? Probably not. Are you the top salesperson in your company? If you're not, then I urge you to take a close and critical look at your own sales behavior. Perhaps there is a bit of the "too busy to sell" salesperson in you.

As customers, we have all encountered this type of salesperson. You have probably reacted the same way most people would. You could hardly wait for them to leave so you could find a "not too busy to sell" salesperson. You may not have analyzed exactly *why* you wanted them to leave, but instinctively you knew you didn't want to do business with them.

Your customers only want from you the same consideration you want when you are the customer.

Chapter 5

MAKE IT EASY AND FUN TO DO BUSINESS WITH YOU!

How many times do you tell your prospects "we can't" or "we don't" or "it's not our policy?" Don't you think it should be your policy to do whatever you can to cultivate customers? Should we "do unto others as we would do unto ourselves?" To do that assumes they want exactly what we want and that's a careless assumption for any business person to make. That's why the fatality rate for the average business is about 78 percent within the first five years. We should do unto our customers as they would have us do unto them.

I once read a survey that the average person has nine dentists. A dentist must have a patient list of 5,000 to have 1,000 active patients. Why is that? Are people in search of a dentist who can do painless dental care?

It costs approximately ten times as much money to get a new customer than it does to keep an existing one. In spite of that, many of us take our existing customers for granted. While we sit back and take them for granted, our competitors are doing everything they can to make our customers their customers. If we all dated our spouses and tried to make the same impression on them we did before we married them, the divorce rate would be drastically reduced. Customers don't want the hassle of finding someone new to deal with. It's a frustrating experience for them.

Just think about how great and painless it is to be able to call the same person every time you need your hair cut. You probably don't spend that much time thinking about it, but wait until that person moves or retires and leaves you having to replace that relationship. It's work to find someone new to cut your hair. Similarly, you want it to be painful and hard work for your customers to replace you. Better yet, you don't want them to even consider replacing you. When a previous client doesn't call you back, do you assume it's their problem? Rest assured, they want the relationship with you to be such that they could call you back.

I have a hot tub that is constantly causing me to call my electrician. I remarked to my wife how fortunate we are to have an electrician who responds to our every call. Once you establish a customer, make sure they are "yours to lose." Allow me to share two of my buying experiences with you.

This Sales Approach Does Not Compute

I began the day as an excited, enthusiastic customer. By the end of the day, I was a worn-out consumer. For months, I knew that I was going to buy a laptop computer for myself for Christmas. I had been window-shopping for a long time. This particular day, however, I was ready to buy, and I put my checkbook in my back pocket before I left the house. I knew where I was going and thought I knew what I was going to buy.

En route to the store where I intended to make my purchase, I stopped off at two others just to confirm my decision. My associate and I had been standing in front of the laptops for only a moment when the salesperson approached us with the old, "Do you have any questions?" I asked him, "Are you the computer expert?" "I know a little bit about them," he said. (That was not what I wanted to hear.) He asked, "What do you want to know?" "Why don't you tell me what you know?" I countered.

This salesperson was off to a poor start. Even his attire did not speak well for him. He had a big tear in one sleeve of his sport coat and a hole in the other. I told myself not to hold that against him. Due to circumstances, some people are not able to make an outward professional impression. Still, I was somewhat surprised the store did not enforce a dress code since it is one of nation's largest and most successful electronics chains. I figured he would make up for it in other areas. He made an attempt to activate several of the computers before finally finding one he could demonstrate. My associate, who knew much more about computers than I did, started going through the programs. The salesperson offered little assistance.

There are steps involved in making a sale (see Chapter 30), sales don't just happen. Either this guy didn't know the steps or didn't care about working through them. After spending approximately ten minutes looking over the displays and another twenty minutes working with the computer, I said, "I'll take this one." The salesperson replied, "Great. I'll go get it." When he came back, he told me they didn't have any in stock. *"A professional salesperson is one who doesn't leave anything to chance."*

A professional salesperson is also one who recognizes the value of his or her time, not to mention that of the customer. Doesn't it make sense to check your inventory prior to making a presentation on a product you don't have? It took all of ten seconds for his computer to show the inventory.

Then he said, "We have one in an open box that has been returned for whatever reason. It has all the warranties of a new one, and we'll knock $100 off the price." "That's fine," I said, "I'll take it." He returned a few minutes later only to say he couldn't find it, but I could have the display model at the same reduced price. When I inquired how old the display was, his response was, "I don't know." Period. No explanation. He did not say, "I don't know. Let me find out." This salesperson (I wish I could think of a more appropriate title for him, because a salesperson he was not) did know at least he was supposed to try to close the sale whether he'd done anything to deserve it or not. He'd learned by now to check inventories and found a store about thirty miles away that showed three in stock. Although he never offered to go get it, he did say I could pay for it at his store and then go pick it up myself. I asked if he worked on commission, and he replied that he did. I asked, since he didn't make any money unless I bought it from him, what incentive had he given me to do business with him. "Since you don't have the product and I'm the one going to pick it up at another store, why should I buy it from you? Are you going to give me a bigger discount since I'm doing all the work?" He said, "I can't do that."

Three questions that must be addressed prior to any sale: (1) Why should the customer buy your product? (2) Why should they buy it from you? and (3) Why should they buy it today? My answers to all three questions had me driving thirty miles to buy one from the other store. When I got there, not only did they not have any, the salesperson could not remember how long it had been since he'd even seen this model. Still, this salesperson was much more enthusiastic and was fun to interact with. He had no trouble selling me on another brand. Guess what happened when he went to get it? That's right, they didn't have it!

For the life of me, I can't understand working to sell something you don't have. He, too, got on the computer and located one. The big difference between this salesperson and the first one was that he was willing to earn his commission. He offered to go get it. I told him I was going to be going in that direction and would pick it up, but he would have to call and make sure they really had one. I wasn't willing to rely on the computer saying that they did. I wanted this guy to have the commission, so I paid for the computer at his store. But what a hassle that turned out to be. It even took ten minutes for the machine to run my check through, at which point I couldn't help but laugh.

Several thoughts ran through my mind, including a quote I had heard years ago. Ira Hayes of National Cash Register had said, "The biggest inflation fighter we have in this country is poor service." I thought how true. I also thought that this experience wasn't really all that unique.

What has happened to business? Has service always been this bad? How can big companies get away with this, when the small ones can't? In many ways, it's depressing to think that this has become the accepted way of doing business. On the other hand, it's encouraging to know that opportunities are unlimited for companies that recognize that service is more than a word. I did finally get my computer at the third store. Because I wanted the product bad enough, I was willing to put up with a bunch of hassles. I had started out on a mission full of excitement and expectations about getting a new product. Five hours later, I had my computer, but my enthusiasm was gone and I was worn out. After all these problems, why did I buy it anyway? Because it was a one-time purchase. Once I wrote my check, I knew I wouldn't have to deal with these salespeople ever again. Had it been a product (such as home remodeling) that would involve an ongoing relationship, those characters would have sent me off in search of someone else from whom to buy. In other words, they made no sale — I *bought* the product from them. They fulfilled the role of an order taker, not a salesperson.

The Long and the Shorts of It

I had quite a different experience when my wife and I decided to spend the extra time we had on an out-of-town business trip doing what she wanted to do. She wanted to shop, which is certainly not my favorite pastime. I must say, however, I can tolerate more of it than most of my male friends. This is largely due to the fact that I'm a people watcher and the shopping malls present a great opportunity for me to do just that. However, on this day, I was going along to shop. I was in the market for a couple pairs of shorts and shirts.

While the first store we went to was far more upscale than where I had intended to shop, it was just right for my wife. I decided, what the heck, I'll look around while she's shopping and, if they have something I like and it's at a super sale price, I'll buy it.

By the time I heard the salesperson ask, "How can I be of help," I had already found a great pair of shorts that were within my budget. I asked if she would help me pick out a shirt that would coordinate with them. I really liked the shirt she showed me, but it cost more than what I had intended to pay for two pairs of shorts and two shirts combined. I told her, "This shirt is way out of my price range. Do people actually buy these? I can't believe anybody would pay that much for a shirt. There is no way I could justify spending that amount of money on just a shirt." The salesperson said in a very relaxed manner, "Yes, we sell quite a few of these shirts and, yes, they are very expensive, but let me tell you why," and she proceeded to give me a terrific sales presentation. I responded, "Well that sounds great, but let's go look at something less expensive." She took some time showing me several other shirts that would also have gone very well with my shorts. However, I was having a difficult time deciding because she had already sold me on that expensive shirt. I really liked it, and those other shirts were just not measuring up.

By this time, the department was getting busy and I was somewhat embarrassed that I was so slow in making a decision. I even told her that she should wait on someone else while I decided what I was going to do. She said, "Oh no, I'm fine. I want to make sure you are happy and get what you want. Let's keep looking." We decided that I should try on the shorts with the three shirts to see which one I liked the best. When I came out of the dressing room, I told her in a jovial manner, "I'm sure this has never happened to you before; but, in my effort to decide which shirts are the best, I have decided to buy all three." (That meant I was buying the shirt that exceeded my entire budget plus two more.) When I paid her for the clothing, she put them in a bag, and then she did something no one has ever done to me in my shopping history. She walked out from behind the counter, handed me my clothes, shook my hand, and said, "Thank you, Mr. Rea. I really enjoyed shopping with you today." I was shocked. I thought to myself, you mean I wasn't a "pain in the butt?" Man, I sure wish I could buy all of my clothing from this person.

As I spent the rest of the day going from store to store with my wife, I couldn't help but pursue two thoughts. First, I wondered if we would still be in this mall if my wife had encountered the same salesperson I had? Second, did I spend all that extra money because I really liked the clothes or because I liked the salesperson? I will often continue to shop after I've already bought something since I'm already in the store anyway, but not this day. I was completely satisfied. I also know how irritable I can become when shopping, but not this day. I wasn't the least bit irritated. I enjoyed myself and didn't begrudge the money I had spent. I had been *sold*. This salesperson told me that, when I wore that nice expensive shirt, I would be noticed. First time out, my wife and I were walking into a restaurant as another couple was walking out.

The lady said, "Nice shirt." This salesperson was still reaping the dividends of a good selling experience.

The salesperson can make the experience. Given the choice, shouldn't you make it enjoyable?

Chapter 6

FINISH STRONGER THAN YOU START

Nearly all salespeople talk a pretty good game. "The proof," as they say, "is in the pudding." Never is your stock or the stock of your company as high as the day you sign the contract with your customer. You need to be ever mindful that there will be days that follow when the customer will question if they should have done this work at all, much less with you.

I had a remodeling contractor call me. A customer wanted his money back after having signed a contract five weeks before. He proceeded to tell me how the guy was nuts. They'd already done part of the work and placed an order for a large portion of the material. He just couldn't understand what was happening. The couple had been so excited about getting this new room addition. I asked what work had been done up to this point. When he informed me that he had put in a skylight, I asked how that had gone. "Well, I sold them a two-by-four skylight; but, when we opened up the area, due to the electrical service they had running all over the place, we could only get a two-by-two in there," he explained. I asked what their reaction was. "They weren't real happy." "Anything else negative I need to know?" I asked. "Well, I told them we could match the wood siding on their house, and now I have found that we can't, and this has them upset, too. They told me everything I've done so far has not been produced the way I told them it would."

"Sounds to me as though the people are justified in asking for their money back," I offered. "They have lost confidence in your ability to perform the job they hired you to do. How would you feel if you were in their place?"

Too often, we, as salespeople, fit the "love 'em and leave 'em" mold. As soon as we get the sale, we figure out what our commission should be on the job, and then we move on in hot pursuit of the next sale.

What could this guy do to get himself back on track with the customer? Perhaps nothing. But the chances are very good that he can salvage the job. I'm sure that he could have put a two-by-four skylight in, although it might have cost him some extra money that he hadn't figured on. Heck, if we put people on the moon, we can put in a skylight. If he truly couldn't, however, he should have at least offered to put the ceiling back the way it was before and refund the money they'd spent on the skylight.

How about the siding match? The contractor was putting on a glass sunroom and said that he didn't see why they were making such a big stink because it was only a little bit of siding. Well, since it was only a little bit, he certainly could have some milled couldn't he? I think this old boy got caught trying to squeeze the deal after he sold it. Shame on him. Unfortunately, what happened to this remodeler is not uncommon.

Too often, we try to do more volume with fewer people or to make more money and deliver less product. As good as that may be in theory, somebody ends up paying — the customer or the contractor or, in most cases, both. We will make enough mistakes and have enough problems without selling somebody short.

A large airline was recently accused of cutting corners in every possible way in an effort to offer the lowest airfares. Things were going great until one of its planes went down, killing all the passengers. Instead of being a company that was concerned only about offering reduced rates, it now found itself fighting for survival. As remodelers, we cut corners occasionally, too. The chances are, however, the corners we cut will not result in the death of someone, but they certainly could. For example, I'm aware of second-story additions falling and improper wiring causing fires, among other things. Granted, these are extreme cases. Most of our cost-cutting practices only cost us money and cause us to become defensive or force us to make apologies we shouldn't have to be making.

That reminds me of a siding mechanic who once worked for me. I called him the "Michelangelo" of siding. I bragged to my prospects that he could conform siding to any piece of wood and make it look as though it had never been covered. Then I encountered a prospect's house that had a lot of ornate trim. Just to be certain I hadn't made a promise I couldn't keep, I took him over to look at the house. He assured me that it would be no problem. While he was there, I had him give me a firm price on doing the job. He said, "The labor will be my standard day rate times twelve days." As it turned out, he grossly underestimated the time that this job would take. He had already spent twelve days on the job before he even started on the customized trim portion.

One morning, I got a call from my customer who said they were not happy with the trim work that had been done the previous day. When I got to the site, I saw why. The work was obviously being done in a way that represented the least amount of effort to the mechanic and did the most to destroy the architectural integrity of the house. When I questioned my man about it, he told me he couldn't figure out a way to cover the trim. I didn't say, "I find it interesting that you could cover it before you started losing money on this job." Instead, I told him, "You are the 'Michelangelo' of siding. Anybody could have covered this trim the way you just did. The reason you are on this job is because of who you are and what you can do. I need you to do what nobody else can do."

When it gets right down to it, many of us have qualities that are more important than making money. Too often, we simply let money cloud our thinking. My "Michelangelo" got back on track and spent an additional ten days doing a beautiful job. Not only was the customer extremely pleased, four of the neighbors so admired the work that they left their names and phone numbers at the job site for me to call them.

A few days later, the customer noticed a couple of things that he thought needed some attention. I agreed and had the mechanic go by to fix them. Then, when I went by to make sure they had been done properly, I could not believe my eyes. Certainly, he had sent a new helper by to make these repairs. The repair work was far worse than the original problem. When I asked the mechanic who had done the work, he said that he had. When I voiced my complaints, he told me he had gone all the way over there without the required materials to make the proper repairs. He had simply done the best he could with what he had and he apologized for taking a shortcut. I didn't feel sorry for him, however.

The job was an hour and a half drive for him each way and now he had to do it again. I wasn't worried about him making the trip though, because I still owed him $3000 as his final payment upon job completion. It wasn't my fault that he had underestimated the job. It also wasn't my fault that he made a bad situation worse having to drive a total of six hours to do a one-hour repair. My responsibility to the customer was to deliver the job I had sold. My responsibility to the siding mechanic was to pay him what I agreed to pay him, not conspire to shortchange the customer.

We all want to make money and, to make money, we have to be concerned about cost. One thing that will get you in trouble every time is: If you sell quality and charge for quality, you'd better deliver quality. Anything less than that makes you a thief!

Chapter 7

DON'T UNDERSELL

"Excuse me sir, but do you have a quarter on you?" That's what I was asked as I came out of the grocery store. I just looked at the beggar standing on the sidewalk. I didn't answer him, but I sure had some thoughts in my head as I walked to my car:

"Yes, I have a quarter. In fact, I have about $200. Why didn't you just ask me for that? Your chances would have been just as good and, in fact, maybe better. When you ask me for a quarter, I know you are a beggar who hopes to hustle enough quarters in a day to buy whatever it is you want to buy. My contribution would be of little significance to you and even less to me. I represent little value to you. In giving you a quarter, I would be doing nothing for you that many before me have not done. By my throwing a quarter in your hat, you have little value to me. What need do you have that I would possibly fill by giving you a quarter? You need a course in Selling 101! Don't you know that all a salesperson wants is a chance to tell their story? You are an order taker who asked a 'yes' or 'no' question that I didn't even give you the courtesy of answering. Have you ever thought about asking for more money? Perhaps an amount that would prompt me to ask, 'What do you need it for?' I know people who have given large sums of money to meet the needs of others. Giving someone a job, a car, or even a house is not out of the question for some. In fact, an anonymous donor just gave a substantial gift to my church, and here you are asking for a quarter. Why not ask for $10? Have you ever figured out how many donors of 25 cents you would have to have to equal just one $10 donor? Forty. And I'll guarantee you that, if I go down the sidewalk and start begging for ten spots, I'll get $10 long before you do at 25 cents a crack. I will have to tell a story though, because I can't stand there like a bump on a log. When folks give me $10, they are going to know why I needed their money. You don't want to work even as a beggar, so you ask for a quarter. I could be where you are someday, so I don't put you down for what you're doing. However, I don't approve of your methods. Can I buy your family a meal? Can I provide you with shelter? I know lots of people. Do you need work? You insult me when you ask me for a quarter when I have so much more to give and am willing to give it if there is a legitimate need. Hey, maybe that's it, there is no need. You're just a con artist. Even so, you'd be a better one if you're asking for at least $10!"

At dinner a few days later, my son, who was a senior in high school at the time, said, "Dad, consider this. I put an ad in *USA TODAY* that reads: 'WANT TO BECOME A MILLIONAIRE? SEND $1.' When people send me the dollar, I tell them to put an ad in the paper just like I did. Do you think I would make any money?" Here we go again, just like the beggar. If my son could tell folks how to become legitimate millionaires, do you think he'd be asking for only one dollar? I think not. Because he'd be offering nothing of value, he'd have to ask for little money.

If you're not getting for your products and services what you need in order to sustain your business and an honest lifestyle, why aren't you? Don't say it's because your clients won't pay you the price you need. More likely, it's because you don't feel you're worth it. You have the mentality that you wouldn't pay yourself that much to do that remodeling job either. Only when you decide you are worth more, will you get more. If you think you're only worth 25 cents, you're going to feel like a crook by asking for $10. When you think you're worth $10, you will stop asking for 25 cents.

Take your inventory. What is your value to a client?

Chapter 8

BUT DON'T OVERSELL EITHER

I have always told my employees, and my children for that matter, to do their best and in most instances that will be good enough. If it isn't good enough, then that's just the way it is. We all can't be everything to everybody. We can't even be everything we would like to be to ourselves. We are not perfect and cannot be, regardless of our desire to be so.

I shouldn't say we are not perfect. If we could hear a playback of some of the comments and promises we make to customers, we would certainly know that the comment "no one's perfect" does not apply to salespeople, especially rookie salespeople.

Do you fit the description of the perfect salesperson who works for the perfect company? You do if you tell your prospects you've never had a dissatisfied client. I really perk up every time I hear salespeople say that. The only way they are telling the truth is if today is their first day on the job. The client knows you're lying, too. You are going to tell me you've been in the remodeling business, a business where you don't even know what you're getting into half the time, and you've never had a dissatisfied client?

There are numerous unknowns in this business. You might open up a wall and find termites or improper wiring. The list of possibilities is endless. You have to now tell your customer, who has stretched their budget to the limit just to afford the new addition, that they are going to have to pay an additional $5,000 before you can proceed. They tell you, "You're the contractor. You should have known. I'm sure this is not the first time you've run into this type of thing." And you expect them to believe you've never had a dissatisfied client? When someone tells me that, I will be listening carefully so I can discern what other lies they might be telling.

I must admit, however, that I went a long time before I ran into the customer I simply could not satisfy...the customer who would not recommend me...the job that left us both hating each other. For every gray hair I gave her, she gave me a stomach cramp. Until I met that client, one of my closing statements went like this, "Mr. and Mrs. Jones, to my knowledge we do not have any customers who are not satisfied with our work. Most are extremely pleased with the work we have done for them. I will admit to you, however, that some of those clients have been harder to satisfy than others and we've had to work extremely hard to satisfy them; but somehow we managed to leave them all satisfied." That comment served me well and let the client know I was not the perfect contractor.

After about eleven years in the business, I had to modify that statement to say, "Mr. and Mrs. Jones, we do a lot of work and have had some wonderful relationships with our customers over the years, but I'll have to say I have had one customer we could not satisfy. I would like to say it was all their fault. I'm sure, however, that we contributed to the problem." Can you see how much more credibility I have by admitting I have a dissatisfied customer rather than saying I have *never* had one? There is the law of diminishing returns here somewhere. In other words, don't go back and count your dissatisfied customers and start bragging that you're celebrating your 253rd dissatisfied customer!

Overselling turns folks off about as quickly as anything you can do. As the song says, "It's hard to be humble when you are perfect in every way." But you'd better find some way to remain humble.

I remember going up against an upstart young remodeler on a room addition. I frankly questioned whether the guy was financially and professionally capable of doing the job. (As it later turned out, he was not.) I was bragging about what a wonderfully successful company we had. We would even be willing to do the work and accept payment upon completion. Then, I sent the customer running to the competition by saying, "I really want your work, but I don't *need* your work. It's not going to affect my economic standard whether I get the job or not." This lady made a comment I will never forget. She said, "I prefer to give my work to someone who needs it." It taught me that, even though I knew my company to be the best, I needed to be very careful about selling it as the best. People like the "underdog" and will often do everything they can to help them. If you are watching a football game and don't know anything about either of the two teams, who do you root for? That's what I thought. I rest my case.

We all say we like winners, but we identify with, and have compassion for, losers. Do you recall the car-rental company that advertised "We're number two. We try harder." That was Avis. I'm convinced that, if they were indeed number two and ever became number one, we would have never known it. They benefited greatly from being in the underdog role. In the eyes of your prospects, sometimes "better" is better than the "best." Muhammad Ali told the world, "If you can do it, it ain't braggin'." That line worked well for Ali, a man whose success depended upon his ability to beat somebody up. Our success, however, depends on how we are perceived. We sell not by boasting about ourselves, but by showing our prospects what others have said about us.

I recently received a call from a smooth-talking phone solicitor out of New York City. I often listen to these folks in hopes of picking up sales tips, and I suggest you do the same. This guy's closing line was, "If I can guarantee you a 300 percent return on your money within six months, would you be interested?" I didn't even have to think about that one. I said, "No, I wouldn't." I'm sure I wasn't the first person to have given him that response, but you certainly would have thought so by his reaction. I told him I would have been much more interested in his proposal, whatever it was, had he asked if I would be interested in a 15 percent return. Sure, 300 percent sounds great. But if I could get a 300 percent return on my money, I wouldn't need to hire phone solicitors to sell the concept. I doubt that I would even want to share the idea with anyone. He oversold me by 285 percent. Get the picture?

Be extremely careful not to oversell.

Chapter 9

DON'T SELL SO CHEAP YOU CAN'T SERVICE YOUR CUSTOMERS

It's one thing to sell your customers something and then not deliver what you sold them. It's an entirely different matter to quote them a price that is so low you can't possibly provide them with the service they deserve. The prospect regards you as the expert, whether you really are or not. Our prospects don't realize that, in most states, just about anybody can become a remodeler. Many assume we all graduated from the Harvard School of Remodeling.

When we give prospects a price, we owe it to them to give them a price that will ensure getting the job done properly. Even when the prospect keeps beating on you to get the price down, they need to be made aware that, while they are doing so, you're mentally deducting quality from the job. It is much less painful in the long run to tell people: "Mr. Jones, we made a decision at my company a long time ago that we would rather explain price than have to apologize for quality. As bad as I want your business, I will not set us both up for failure. I priced this job where it needs to be in order to deliver to you the quality and craftsmanship that you want and deserve and that has earned us the reputation we enjoy. The salesperson in me wants to do whatever it takes just to get the job. But don't put me in a position where I'm trying to determine ways where my company can cut quality without you noticing a difference. Mr. Jones, that's not fair to you or to me." Most of the time, that little speech is appreciated, and the prospect views you as the type of contractor with whom they want to deal. More often than not, they can come up with the extra money that's needed. If they don't, then get up, walk out, and don't look back.

I learned a very valuable lesson in the car business: Never sell someone too cheaply to service them. We would sometimes get beat up so badly on the price of a used car, we would finally say, "Okay, you've got a deal, but, at that price, it's *as is*." When someone has a breakdown on the way home, or the battery goes dead the first week, you quickly find out that the customer has no concept of what an *as is* warranty really is, even though you may have explained it in great detail. They may even have signed a document stating this car was sold *as is*. A lot of people will take a chance because they think nothing is going to go wrong. If something does go wrong, they still want service. Now, try to explain to someone that they didn't pay enough to get service.

The person who died and didn't buy the life-insurance policy you tried to sell them might later be sorry, but the good news is they're not around to berate you for your lack of sales ability. This is not true for the car salesperson or the remodeler. You're going to hear them complain that you sold them on your product but now you're denying service. It's a "no win" situation for you. You sold them the job without the "service factor" built into the price, and now the product needs service. And, if you don't provide some service, the customer is going to bad-mouth you to everybody they know. You can be assured they'll neglect to tell people that they purchased the product *as is*.

The lady who cuts my hair is a real success. I have tremendous respect for her work ethic, and I just marvel when watching her work. The key to her success is not only that she's a great time manager, but that she also gives great service and has a genuine appreciation for her customers. She told me how she and about twenty members from her family went to a nice restaurant for Mother's Day. When her meal came, the meat was not prepared as she had ordered and so she asked them to put it back on the grill. When the meal finally came back, it was burned. The other members of her family were now finished eating. She told the waitress that she couldn't eat the burned meat and, besides, the kids were getting restless and running all over the restaurant. She said she'd appreciate it if they would just take her meal off the bill. The waitress said, "I can't do that. You'll have to talk with the manager." The manager caused even more problems, so the owner was brought in to settle the issue. He said, "I'll settle this thing." He asked her, "How much of the meat did you eat?" "None." "Fine, I'll deduct the full price of the meat." "Did you eat any of the vegetables?" "No." "Then I'll deduct the price of the vegetables." "Did you eat any of your salad?" "Yes" "Okay, the salad is $2.50." "How about a drink, did you drink anything?" "Yes, I had a soft drink." "Okay, that's $1. Your total is $3.50 plus tax."

If you were the owner of that restaurant what would you have done? This is one of the nicest restaurants in our area and one of the most expensive. They were not only humiliating a customer, they were nickel-and-diming her to death. You've heard it said, "Never let a dime hold up a nickel." Well, this takes the cake (no, she didn't have dessert!). The restaurant put $3.50 in the cash register. Big deal! Every person in this group of twenty was aware of the unprofessional manner in which the owner responded. My hairstylist told me and, I'm sure, most of her other customers.

What should the restaurant owner have done? First of all, he should have said the two words that are so rarely used but will satisfy just about any complaint you will ever get: "I'm sorry" (see Chapter 28). Then, at a minimum, he should not have charged her one cent for her meal. He then should have given her his business card and written on the back "good for any meal on the menu, anytime." This way, he gets his money back giving away one meal, because the odds of someone eating alone are slim. He knows that, too. So, if he really wants to do something nice, he gives her a meal for two.

Anybody can sell a product. Service is what keeps customers. Smart companies recognize the best advertising dollars they can possibly spend are those spent in making an unhappy customer happy. It was no secret that my remodeling company was one of the highest-priced companies in town. Unlike many of my competitors, who became overly defensive when their prices were questioned, I took a great deal of pride in explaining why we were expensive. As long as my customers kept a "but" in the sentence I was happy: "Phil's high *but* he's worth it." "Phil's high *but* his company does excellent work." "Phil's expensive *but* with him you get what you pay for."

I was walking through a shopping mall one evening in the late 1970s. The nation's economy was in bad shape and interest rates were in the low twenties. I noticed about one out of every ten stores in this mall was closed or in the process of closing. Upon closer examination, I saw that all these failing businesses were the low-price, cut-rate type of stores that sold nothing but price. The nicer, more expensive stores seemed to be doing just fine. Was it because they had charged enough money to carry them through periods of bad times? I don't think so. Rather, I think they recognized that folks with money have money in both good times and bad and, if they choose to sell to that clientele and more importantly provide service to that clientele, they would be able to maintain a profitable business. I wonder what will happen to that restaurant when the economy has another severe downturn.

You make money in the long run by making people happy, not by having them leave with the intent of never coming back. How many times have you put a little money in the cash register and considered yourself the winner?

The customer is always right, even when they are wrong.

Chapter 10

YOUR COMPETITION WILL HELP YOU BY NOT WORKING!

In the acting profession, they say, "Go on this audition as if it were your last audition. If you don't, it just might be." This is good advice for the salesperson as well. You need to go on every sales call prepared to make that sale. Being prepared means having samples of any and everything you think the prospect might want or need to see. If your samples are not in good working or presentable order, then don't show them. Having samples will often give you a huge selling advantage because many of your competitors will not.

You get jobs by doing your job. You also get jobs because other salespeople didn't do their job. It's said that only 17 to 20 percent of all salespeople even ask for the business. It's also said that it takes five closes to sell the job. I'm sure you have gone in to make a presentation and done very little work and still the prospect said, "Just write up the contract." The chances are good that someone before you took this prospect right to the brink of making a decision and did not finish the job by asking them for the order. Producing a sale requires some effort on your part. Some sales require more effort than others. Don't fail to get the job just because you didn't work to get it.

Some salespeople want the close without the effort. The good ones do make it look very easy, just as the professional golfer does. Few of us are aware of how many hours of hitting one golf ball after another it takes to get good enough to make a living at it.

When my son was fifteen years old, I took him on two appointments with me. I was fortunate enough to sell them both. I was proud that my son had seen his dad displaying his skill and could hardly wait for my son's response. On the way home, he said, "Dad, that's all you do? That was so easy!" After taking a minute to compose myself, I said, "Ryan, do you remember when the first client said, 'We'll think about it and get back with you?'" Ryan said, "Yes." "I have a contract though, don't I?" I continued. "Do you remember the second client saying they were going to get other estimates and I said, 'But I have a contract, don't I?'"

It's better to go on those appointments preparing for opportunity that never comes than have opportunity come and not be prepared.

Chapter 11

NOW HEAR THIS! LISTENING PAYS BIG DIVIDENDS

If you will only listen, people will tell you how to sell them. As salespeople, we cannot quite get it through our heads that listening pays better than talking. We think a selling job is a talking job. If you talk long enough, you are more apt to eventually say the wrong thing instead of the right thing. If I promised you that you could increase your income by 20 to 50 percent by working on your listening skills, would you at least make an effort to listen?

I'm often amazed at the comments I hear prospects make that I think the salesperson has ignored only to find out later that they did not hear the prospect at all. When I go out as an observer on sales calls, I admit I'm at a tremendous advantage. I'm not directly involved in the conversation. Therefore, all I have to do is listen. I don't have to think about what I'm going to say next while the customer is talking. I just listen. It rarely fails that people will tell you how to sell them. Even when they say, "We want you to know we're getting other estimates," or "We're just looking around," or "We're not ready to buy now," or "We always talk among ourselves before we make final decisions." The prospect is telling you what has to take place for the sale to happen.

For the person who wants other estimates, you can provide them estimates on more than one product yourself. Give them a choice. For the person who wants to look around, you take them to look around. Schedule appointments with some of your previous customers to show off your work to your new prospects. I do not ever recall, nor do most of my seminar participants recall, not selling a job when they took prospects to previous customers' homes. We don't do it enough. What are we going to do with those folks who want to talk about the purchase without you present? Give them that opportunity. After you've finished your presentation, ask if they have any questions and, once their questions have been addressed, say, "You expressed the need to talk this over, and I want to give you that opportunity." Then go to your car to do paperwork, go check on another job, go eat lunch, whatever — just check back with them in thirty to sixty minutes. Is this exactly what the folks had in mind? Probably not. Ask yourself, how long do you and your spouse talk over something before making a decision? My seminar surveys over the years show the longest response to be thirty minutes. Do these techniques work? They sure do. Do they work all the time? They sure don't. That's another discovery I noticed about salespeople: If a technique isn't 100 percent successful, that's it, it doesn't work. I can promise you it will never work if you never try it.

I went on a sales call with a salesperson named Ed. It was on a relatively small job. It had been Ed's custom to gather the information and then come back to the office, figure the job, and then mail the estimate. This prospect was true to form, giving Ed all the sales-closing ammo he needed. Ed's problem was that he wasn't experienced enough to realize it. The prospect said he'd talked with another company by phone. When they said they couldn't do the work for at least five weeks, he'd told them not to even bother coming. What should this have told Ed? Certainly, this person had a sense of urgency. So when he was asked how long it would be before he could get started, he said, "Four weeks." I thought I was going to die! The customer had just told a guy with a five-week backlog not to even bother coming over. I didn't expect Ed to lie, but I would have expected him to say it differently (see Chapter 14). Rather than saying he couldn't start for four weeks, he could have said, "Mr. Jones, we will begin the work when I leave here this afternoon. We'll begin the permit process, get the material list, and make sure we have all the materials on hand so we can minimize delays once we begin the project."

As bad as Ed had messed that up, the worst was yet to come. When he was figuring the cost of the job, he told Mr. Jones that he wasn't accustomed to doing it by hand, because he usually figured costs on his computer. To which Mr. Jones said, "Well I hope that computer has not gotten up to $2,000 yet." A few minutes later, Ed handed me the proposal to review. The price at the bottom read $1,305. I changed the "three" to a "five." Not only could Ed have charged more for the job, the job was worth more. (I had actually wanted to change the "three" to an "eight" but was fearful of blowing Ed's mind.)

When Ed gave the price, Mr. Jones said, "$1,505. That much?!" in a loud, surprised manner. Mr. Jones was playing the role of the customer and playing it well. He knew not to show how pleasantly surprised he was. The salesperson could have said, "Well, I could knock off a little bit." Ed, however, had the right response when he said, "Mr. Jones, that's a lot of work for that amount of money." Mr. Jones said, "Okay, I've got a few more things I'd like to add." Ed eventually got most of the $2,000 that Mr. Jones had told him earlier that he had to spend. I'm not telling you, or even suggesting to you, that you charge someone $2,000 for a $1,000 job even if they tell you that's their budget. What I am saying is it is ridiculous to cut yourself down to the penny, take all the risk, figure no contingency, and then shake in your shoes when you present a price of $1,305 when the customer thinks a fair price for the project is $2,000. In this case, the customer did a better job of estimating the value than Ed did.

A salesperson is one who offers goods or services in exchange for money. Most salespeople have a variety of goods and services they can offer. To determine what "to show and tell," you must listen to your prospect. The salesperson who talks the most frequently loses the sale to the one who listens the best. Are you impressed by how much you know and then try to impart that knowledge to others? Or do you listen so you can recommend the proper remedy? I heard a statistic that 80 percent of male physicians interrupt their patients while they're describing their symptoms after fifteen seconds or less and female physicians listen only slightly longer. As a salesperson, you can make the money physicians make, but you'd better listen a lot longer than they do.

Listen for information that will give you direction to make the sale. It's there.

Chapter 12

YOU CAN MAKE MONEY BY ACCIDENT, BUT YOU CAN'T SAVE IT BY ACCIDENT

You can make money by accident. You can win a lottery and be an instant millionaire. Your rich aunt may leave you her estate. Heck, even most successful business people don't set out to get rich. They set out trying to provide for their families. But it's not by accident they got rich. In all likelihood, they offered a good service at a fair price.

Regardless of how it happens, when you have money come your way, you need to make a conscious decision on what you are going to do with it. Money will not deposit itself into your 401K plan or into your mutual funds. You will need to put it there. As a good professional salesperson, you will make money. It comes with the territory. Whether money is a high priority to you or not, it is a by-product of the good job you do. The money will roll in. You should decide, before you make it, what you are going to do with it. Look at lottery winners. You've heard people say, "If I ever won a lottery, I would do everything just as I am doing now. Nothing would change, except I would pay off some bills, maybe get a new car, but I wouldn't quit my job." You've later seen television shows depicting how many of those same lottery winners are now flat broke.

Salespeople, too, are notorious for being "high rollers" one minute and consulting with bankruptcy lawyers the next. I converted a carpenter into sales in the early 1980s. As a carpenter, he'd been making about $15,000 a year. In his first full month in sales, he made $8,000. He immediately went out and bought a very expensive vehicle. In less than six months, it was repossessed.

You stand a better chance of making money when you plan to make money. You can, however, make it without planning, and you sure can spend it without planning. But you will never ever save it without planning. I bet that's why it is referred to as a "savings *plan*" by banks.

My dad used to say, "Son, it's never how much you make, it's how much you save. People fall into one of two categories, they're either spenders or savers." Oh, I don't mean a spender doesn't save or a saver doesn't spend, but, when it gets right down to it, they delight in one more than the other. My parents were savers, big time. My mother was a social worker for the government, and my father was an agricultural extension agent (a government employee who provided advice to farmers). The most either one of them ever made was $21,000 per year. Yet, when my father passed away, he left an estate worth several million dollars. That would have had a much greater impact on me if I hadn't had four brothers and sisters! Seriously, my folks saved an enormous amount of money in spite of having five children. They had the usual expenses of any large family, plus they provided dental braces for two, had three in college at one time, etc.

I don't know how in the world my parents did so much with so little and still saved money. I really do know how they did it. I just don't know why I don't do as well with much more. My parents both got a great deal of enjoyment from saving money. The fact that both were so good at saving is extremely odd. I have done credit applications on couples for more than twenty-five years, and I could always tell which spouse was the spender and which was the saver. Rarely did I leave with the conclusion that both were savers. On the contrary, I often surmised that both were spenders, an assessment that was often reinforced when the bank would turn them down for being financially over-extended.

My parents shared with me their simple financial plan early on: the good old "work one week for yourself" plan. Even today, I can hear them saying, "Phil, no matter how much money you make or how little, always work one week for yourself. Live within your means so that you can meet all your obligations on three weeks' worth of pay and save the fourth week. Of the first three weeks, use one for shelter, one for food, and one for other obligations. If you stick with this throughout your working life, barring any catastrophe, you should be all right."

That plan doesn't work that easily for a commission salesperson. One week, I may make lots of money, and, the next week, I may not make any. That's what happened to my old sales rep with the new car. He had a positive attitude that he was going to make at least as much every month as he'd made in his first month. In fact, that's the way many sales organizations motivate their employees, by encouraging them to buy something bigger and better so they will have to make more money to pay for it.

Working for bigger and better eventually gets old, I can assure you. The term is "burnout." It's a game you can never ever win. You may catch up, and you may even keep up for awhile, but at some point you get tired.

If you're new to the selling profession, continue to live on your present budget. Don't adjust your lifestyle based on the money you're going to be making or even the money you may already be making. Make sure your new level of income becomes the norm and not the exception before you commit yourself to new financial obligations. I can't tell you how many potentially good salespeople I have seen overcommit themselves early in their selling careers and put so much financial pressure on themselves that they had to return to lower-paying, yet guaranteed, salary positions to relieve that pressure. As a newly commissioned salesperson, you can easily make $10,000 one month and $1,500 the next. That, however, is still $11,500 in two months. Chances are that, as a salaried employee, you'd make much less than that in a two-month period. It takes a concentrated and dedicated effort to live within your means.

Late one Saturday afternoon when I was in the car business, our dealership got swamped with a flood of people. As it turned out, a large national multilevel marketing company was having a convention in town, and it had just adjourned. The customers I waited on were a very nice couple who both held good, solid, blue-collar jobs with our area's largest employer. They told me how they had committed to working part-time with this organization and had just participated in a rally that left them extremely excited and motivated about the financial opportunities. They had been told, "If you want to acquire something, go out and buy it, and then you will make the money to pay for it." They were told, "Without the pressure on you to perform, you rarely will." Well, they bought the biggest, nicest, most expensive car on the lot. It was a very enjoyable and lucrative sale for me.

About a year later, a wrecker pulled in with their car in tow and proceeded to put it in our repossessions line. I got a real bad feeling. I had done my job as a salesperson. Who was I to tell a couple almost twice my age that they were overspending? As sales professionals, we can't read people's minds. Even knowing that, I still felt sorry for the couple. They had been caught up in the hype of the day and made a premature decision that undoubtedly ended up causing them many hours of stress and worry. The multilevel company had not wronged them. It was, and still is, one of the most successful organizations in our country, having made millionaires out of lots of people who shared the same vision my customers had. My point is, make the money before you start spending it.

All of us have pressure on us to sell. If you think you don't, just stop selling and see what happens. I have, however, found that the easiest time for me to make a sale is right after I just made one. The reason is that I've already made my sale for the day and there's no pressure to make another one. You have heard that "the rich get richer" and "it takes money to make money." The days when the pressure is not on you to perform are the days you most often give your best performance.

One more of my Dad's favorite sayings: "The sun does not shine on the same dog all the time." Plan for rainy days, plan for vacations, and plan for retirement.

Don't assume you will just make the money you need when the need arises.

Chapter 13

WORK YOUR CUSTOMERS, NOT YOUR COMPANY AND SUPPLIERS

It's been said that every time a salesperson and a potential customer come together a sale takes place. Either the customer sells the salesperson or vice versa.

I remember a particular time when it became obvious that the customer was a better salesperson than I was. It was back in my car business days. The manager had appraised the man's trade-in and given me the figure that it would take to make the deal. I went back into my office full of confidence that what my boss was asking was fair and reasonable and was certain my customer and I were going to be able to finalize the deal. For the next ten minutes after I presented the figure, the man proceeded to give me all the reasons why he couldn't go beyond a certain amount, which added up to be several hundred dollars below the amount my boss wanted for the car. He made it clear that, while he thought my boss was being fair, it was just not something he could do. I got up, went back out to the boss and told him why my customer could not exceed his amount. I was aware of the profit margin that was involved and knew that we could make a deal even at the amount the customer had offered. When I finished telling the boss the story in my most convincing manner, he said, "Now, go back and work the customer as hard as you're trying to work me." That remark really made an impression on me. He was right — I was trying to work the guy who was on my side, the guy who wrote my paycheck, the guy who provided me with many benefits, including a paid vacation. Why was I trying to convince him to take less than he deserved? And why was I disappointed that he wasn't buying my story? It boiled down to the fact that I was more comfortable working the boss. It was easier, or so I thought. It also certainly provided less money for me.

As commissioned salespeople, we all know that the more we get for our products, the more money we make. I certainly wanted to be fair with the customer and wanted to give him good service in hopes that he would make future purchases from me and refer me to others, but my allegiance should have been to my employer. I was fooling myself. I did not have the power to make the customer do anything he didn't want to do. He was there to represent himself, and I was hired to represent the company. In the twenty-plus years since hearing that remark, I have been quick to recognize when other salespeople are working their company or suppliers.

A building contractor will practically beg a painter to reduce his price by $100, whether he has given full price for his project or not. That's just part of the deal — beat up on the suppliers, subcontractors, whatever you have to do to get the price down. These are people we like, too. These are the people with whom we have chosen to associate our businesses. Rather than work the customer in the manner we should, we choose to work our associates. Never mind that this could be the only dealing we ever have with the customer, and we deal with our suppliers and contractors daily.

Taking the easiest, simplest route with the customer, and then putting the squeeze on everybody else down the line to make the deal work doesn't appear to make a lot of sense.

Chapter 14

CAN NO COMMUNICATIONS BE BETTER THAN SOME?

Over the past twenty years, more seminars and more books have been written on communication than perhaps any other subject. What can be more important than to be able to express ourselves and to be understood the way we want to be understood? The ability to communicate effectively is an integral part of our professional and personal lives.

My family left home early to catch a 6:30 a.m. flight. The early hour didn't bother any of us, as we were all excited about our Disney World vacation. Our plane left a little late, enough to make me nervous about making our 8:30 a.m. connecting flight. After hurrying to make our connections, we saw this sign over the desk at the gate: "DELAYED. NOW DEPARTING 9:00 a.m." Nine o'clock came, and we had not heard anything. At 9:30, I walked up to the desk, and the departing time had been changed to 11:00. Just prior to 11:00, I walked up to the desk along with several other disgruntled passengers. I asked the attendant, "What's the story?" All she said was, "I don't know." "Would you mind checking with someone who does know?" She said, "Nobody knows." I was still surprisingly calm, but I was starting to get somewhat irritated at this point. I noted, "Those departing times are not changing by themselves. Either you or someone else is changing them and must have some reason. All I'm asking is that you communicate with us. This departure has been delayed now three times without one word of explanation." She said, "Okay, I'll make an announcement."

Before I could get back to my seat, this is what I heard, "Ladies and gentlemen, this aircraft is on its way over to the gate now. This plane was scheduled for departure to Orlando last night at 8:30. During routine maintenance, a problem was detected. It should now be a safe plane." It *should* be a safe plane? What in the world does she mean it *should* be a safe plane? What started with a simple lack of communication ended as extremely poor communication. In this case, I would have felt better with no communication.

I'm Positive You Shouldn't be Negative

When we finally got on the plane, a man walked over to the gentleman seated in front of us and said, "You wouldn't change seats with me, would you? — So I can sit with my family?" This person had a very easy request, but he made it hard for the person to give him the answer he wanted. "You wouldn't, would you?" The obvious response would be, "No, I wouldn't." I'm surprised how many folks communicate negatively in search of a positive response. Doesn't this sound better?: "Sir, would you be kind enough to exchange seats with me so I can sit with my wife and daughter?" Answering "yes" means I will be kind, while answering "no" means I will not be kind. Granted there are some mean folks out there, but I'll get more positive responses that way than with "you won't, will you?"

My friend and golfing partner, Lon, can hit everybody's driver but his own. He is always asking others with whom we play, "Do you mind if I hit one with your driver?" He likes everyone else's better than his own, too. Recently, however, he hit with one he really liked. The owner of the club told him he was welcome to use it through the rest of the round. After several holes, Lon said, "I sure like that driver, I wonder if he will sell it." On the final hole Lon decided, "I'm going to ask him if he will sell it to me." I asked, "Lon, do you want the driver?" He said, "Yes, I really do." I said, "Then don't ask him if he will sell it, because he can say yes or no. Ask him how much he will take for it." Lon took my advice and did exactly what I said. Guess what? The guy *gave* him the driver, and Lon has been beating me ever since!

My brother Kyle has been in the real-estate business for a number of years. In a recent phone conversation, I asked him how business was. He told me how he had made a mistake the day before and lost a listing he was sure he had. He was talking with the prospect over the phone when he was asked about doing an "open house" as a tool to market his home. Kyle responded without hesitation that he hadn't done an "open house" in ten years. When Kyle called him back to do the paperwork on the listing, the prospect had already listed with someone else. I can assure you it was someone who does "open houses."

Kyle admittedly made a communication mistake. We all make them. However, knowing that we do is our greatest ally. Kyle did not say he wouldn't do an "open house," he simply said he had not done one in ten years. The prospect could not have cared less when Kyle did his last one. Kyle could have said a number of things that could have acquired the listing for him, such as: "Mr. Prospect, when would be a good time for us to meet to discuss the best strategy for your home?" I would be willing to bet that, had Kyle said what he said to the prospect face-to-face, he would have been able to read his expression and would have known immediately that he'd said something the prospect did not want to hear.

I don't know where people get these statistics, but this is one I don't have any trouble believing: Effective communication is 7 percent verbal, 38 percent tone of voice, and 55 percent visual (body language).

Anything you say to a prospect that you deem as important, a potential deal-making or deal-breaking statement, you'd better be there to see their response.

Chapter 15

YOU DON'T HAVE TO PLAY THE HAND YOU'RE DEALT

One of the wonderful benefits of being a remodeling salesperson is that we can choose our clients. That's right, we don't have to do business with everyone. We can pick and choose based on whether we like the folks, whether we feel they are going to be good to work with or a pain in the you know what. You can ask yourself if this is the type of job for which you and your company are well suited. Although your company can probably do the job, does it seem to be one that will fit your profit structure? How many times have you taken a job and just hoped there would be some money at the end? Not all business is good business.

Good salespeople are capable of selling lots of work, even work they don't want or need. They know they have the ability to sell the jobs they want to sell. This is not the case with the order taker who consistently brings in undesirable and non-profitable jobs. The order taker writes up any contract the customer will sign. That is precisely why when I ask remodelers, "How's business?" — more often than not, they reply, "Oh, business is good. We've got more than we can do." I then ask if they are meeting their financial goals. Few ever are. It stands to reason that, if a company has more work than they can do, they should be making more money than they can spend.

We are very fortunate to be able to selectively choose our clientele. The furniture dealer, for example, doesn't have that option. Even though the customer may seem like they will be a "pain" to deal with, the only way the furniture dealer cannot do business with them is to say, "I don't want your business." Not exactly what you want to go around telling people.

In our business, there are many avenues we can take when we don't want a particular person as a client. The one many of you use, more often by accident than design, is to tell the people you will work up the estimate and get back with them and then simply never get back with them. By the time you get to your car, you've already determined that they'll never hear from you. Or, you ask folks how soon they would like to have the work done and then tell them there is no way you could possibly get to it by then. Or, you give them a price that is twice what your regular price is and figure if you get the job, you're being paid well for the anticipated aggravation.

You have to be careful with "negative selling." This occurs when you don't want the job. You say things that you know will discourage the prospect from using you. However, the more negative you are, the more they are drawn to you. That principle worked well during my dating days. I couldn't get a date when I went after one, but the girls in whom I had no interest were always attracted to me. It took a lot of discipline for me to act nonchalant with the girls in whom I was really interested. Negative selling is very powerful when you know what you are doing.

Knowing When to Take a Hike

How do you know when to walk away from prospective clients? You already know. You just need to trust your instincts. How many times have you finished a job and said afterwards, "I knew that guy was going to be a jerk the first time I met him"? The signs are almost always there from the beginning. On the other hand, we don't want to be overly sensitive and look for reasons not to do business with people.

Sorry, but there is no perfect customer, because there are no perfect people. When their house is all torn to pieces and their family of five is forced to share one bath while your job is two weeks beyond your completion date, you will find that they are even less perfect than you may have thought.

I was sitting on a porch with a prospect and was getting out the contract when he said, "I sure hope you are as good as you say you are because I now have suits pending against Sears and Penney's." I thought to myself, "We're good, but I know Sears and Penney's to be darn good, credible companies." Don't fool yourself into thinking that you can satisfy somebody whom both Sears and Penney's couldn't. I walked away from that one.

Another time, I was in the office of a prospect who happened to be an attorney. I had signed a contract with him after what had been a long and difficult period of negotiating and nit-picking. When he gave me the deposit check, he said, "I want you to know I expect this job to be perfect." I handed the check back to him and told him we should have terminated our relationship long before getting to this point. We were both worn out. I had persisted in the process because I felt like I had invested too much time and energy into getting the job to stop (okay, my sales ego temporarily clouded my judgment).

I suggested he find someone else to do the work, because it's impossible for me to deliver a perfect job. I told him that if I had conveyed that impression, then I had oversold my abilities along with the abilities of my company. I no longer wanted the job and can tell you that I felt a great deal of relief that I wasn't going to be doing it. That feeling of euphoria, however, didn't last long. The attorney was a better salesperson than I was, and he talked me into moving forward. He assured me that we would have a good working relationship. The job was an absolute nightmare. At the end, I hated him and he hated me. I gave up much of my anticipated profit and gained some more unneeded gray hairs in the process.

We've all had those types of clients and, as long as we stay in business, we're going to have more. The key is to minimize them. How much complaining do you hear the prospect doing about others? I would always say, "Mr. and Mrs. Jones, let me ask you, can you be satisfied? Because frankly there are people who cannot. If you can be satisfied, then we have the products and the personnel to satisfy you. If, however, you are one of those folks who, no matter what you get, will feel there is something wrong with it, we'll be no different, and it would be better for us both to deal with that issue now."

The one "real bad" experience I had with my "real bad" client gave me the nerve to make that little speech on a number of occasions. I'm convinced it saved me from having a similar experience. It lessened perhaps unrealistic expectations on the customer's part. I don't recall it ever costing me a job. But, if it had, that would have been okay, too. I never ever wanted to go through the emotional pain and sleepless nights I experienced for months dealing with that "real bad" client.

A good salesperson doesn't have to play the cards they're dealt. They are confident enough to not only get a new deck, but to find someone else with whom to play.

Chapter 16

DISCIPLINE HAS TO BE IN THERE SOMEWHERE

My wife asked who wanted the last taco. When none of my children answered, she said, "Phil eat this last taco." "I don't want it," I said. "Oh come on, I don't want to throw it out." "Okay, bring it over here." My son chimed in, "Dad, you don't have any discipline, do you?"

My definition of discipline is making yourself do something you don't want to do in order to achieve something you do want to achieve. How could he possibly say to me that I don't have any discipline? I get up before 6:00 every morning. On Mondays, Wednesdays, and Fridays, I do a two-hour workout at the gym. On Tuesdays and Thursdays, I run seven miles and, on Saturdays, up to eighteen miles. On Sundays, I ride my bike anywhere from fifteen to thirty miles. Does he have any idea how much discipline it takes to do that? Many mornings, I wake up tired, not feeling well, certainly not feeling motivated to start the day out in pain. I have discipline. In response to my son's question, I told him, "Son, I have discipline in many areas of my life and none in some other areas. Fortunately, the areas where I do have discipline offset those where I don't, such as exercising versus eating. If I didn't exercise the way I do and still continued my current eating habits, I would have a whole other set of problems, and my lack of discipline would be obvious to everyone."

Most of us are in the same situation. We sacrifice in one area so we can be extravagant in others. Thank goodness we don't have to be disciplined in all areas of our lives. But we do have to have it in some areas. It is extremely important for you to do an inventory of your personal work habits. Where are your strengths? Where are your weaknesses? Do your strengths compensate for your weaknesses? How willing are you to do those things that you don't want to do, but know will be good for you? In other words, how committed are you? How disciplined are you?

I know for a fact that the best, most profitable, and the least expensive lead to get in the remodeling business is to go knock on someone's door. I know because I did it for four hours nearly every day for four years. There was little, if any, competition for the business I was getting. I was often able to recognize needs just by walking up to the house. Based on what I saw, I could often create a sense of urgency. Most folks, certainly the ones who bought from me, liked me, trusted me, and found no reason to call someone else. As easy and as profitable as it was, did I like doing it? No. Every day, I looked for reasons not to go out knocking doors. It's too hot, too cold, too early in the day, too late in the day, too dangerous, too many dogs out there, too many folks don't want to be bothered, etc. Finding an excuse was not a problem. Getting started was. Once I did get started, though, it became enjoyable. It provided a level of confidence to see all those homes that needed work. It was a good feeling to know that I was not sitting back waiting for things to happen, but instead working to make things happen. Where is your lack of discipline, in prospecting, closing, collecting? It's certainly to your advantage if you can directly work on your areas of weakness and not depend on an area of strength to compensate for them. Selling is not a single-focused profession. It is made up of many acts, not all of which you will enjoy. It will take discipline on your part to perform those acts, but you can do it.

Discipline is making yourself do something you don't want to do in order to achieve something you want to achieve. Where do you need discipline to achieve the level of success you want to acquire as a remodeling salesperson?

Chapter 17

EVERY JOB MUST BE ABLE TO STAND ALONE

When I was in the automobile business, people would often trade in their old car on a new one. It was not unusual for us to take in a trade that was extremely difficult to sell. The company policy was that, if a trade-in became ninety days old and it was still unsold, you sold it to a wholesaler. Now, if we couldn't sell it to a retail customer, how could we sell it to a wholesaler who made a living buying cars from one dealer and selling them to another dealer? There were two ways to do it: (1) Take your loss, or (2) package the car with several others you had taken in at the right price and that were marketable. This would get rid of the loser, but it sure robbed us of the potential profit on the other cars. To make matters worse, it was rare that one other car would offset the loss, normally it took two or three. Not only did someone at the dealership make a mistake in judgment (we never took in a car to lose money on it), but every month the car sat on the lot, it depreciated. While we lost money on some cars, the name of the game was to minimize the losses.

Remodelers don't often work that way. They take a job at a loss or low margin in hopes of getting a more profitable job from the customer down the road. In hopes that their profit will come from change orders. In hopes that it will be good advertising. In hopes that working in certain neighborhoods will change their public image. Hope is nice, but it doesn't make a remodeling company profitable.

I was having dinner with a remodeler who had just sold a $700,000 job. He was all smiles. When I asked him what he anticipated making on this job, he said he didn't know. So I asked him what he hoped to make. His response was $30,000. I almost fell off my chair when I thought of having that kind of exposure for just $30,000 profit. I didn't ask him to explain his reasoning, because I was scared it might make sense to me. Think about it. You could clean windows, gutters, or mow lawns and make that much money in the same amount of time it would take to do a $700,000 renovation — and with no exposure.

I thought that was bad until I got a newsletter from a remodeler whom I'd never met but had talked with several times on the phone. He makes good sense and produces a wonderful newsletter. An article in his publication prompted me to call him immediately. It told of a $1.2 million project that his company had just finished. The article described how proud they were of the final results and how happy the customers were. I called and left the following message in his voice-mail: "Tell me how much you anticipated making and how much you actually made."

Take a moment and consider what your absolute minimum expected profit would be on a job of that size. I said *expected* profit. Going into a $1.2 million job and not taking into account some catastrophic occurrence that could possibly cost you money, how much would you expect to profit?

I know that, for me, the profit would have to be $300,000. That would mean the job would cost me $900,000. If I'm subbing out most of the work and it's not tying up any of my workforce for a year, okay, maybe $200,000, but not a dime less. You might think $200,000 sounds like a huge number, but that's a gross markup of less than 20 percent. Can you make it on a 20 percent markup? I don't think so. Don't let the $200,000 blind you. Never mind my minimum profit number, what was yours?

The contractor who sold the job told me he went into it planning to make $60,000, but had only made $30,000 because "rich people are hard to please." I would say he did a pretty good job if he only spent $30,000 of his anticipated profit on a $1.2 million job pleasing someone. The most pathetic part of the whole deal was taking a job of that magnitude and hoping to make $60,000 — that's only 5 percent! The end result was actually 2.5 percent. That's less than any state sales tax I've ever paid on a product.

Granted, I don't know all the details behind that particular job, but I do know it costs you a certain amount for every dollar of volume you put on your books. Many items associated with your business are tied into your volume such as, workers' compensation, liability insurance, business licensing, taxes, etc. If you factor these items into that job, the contractor *might* have enough left over to buy a soft drink.

He said he would have to chalk it up to $50,000 worth of advertising. That's still not close to where the profit should be. If you want $50,000 worth of advertising, there are far better ways to get it than by doing a $1.2 million renovation on someone's home. Those customers told him they would be glad to let him show prospects their home. After about the third time he calls asking to show it, they will likely say, "No thanks."

This contractor did not make an intelligent decision when he sold this job. However, if he were not an intelligent contractor, he would be out of business. Not many companies could have done this job and survived to tell about it. Even fewer would have left behind a happy customer. It's a fact of life for most business people that, when they see the profit from a job is gone, so are they. Every contractor eventually does a job from which they learn to say, "I'll never do that again!" My advice is to learn that from a little job, not a million-dollar one that takes a year to complete. That's a big — and potentially very expensive — learning curve.

A few days after I talked with this contractor, I had lunch with a friend who is a sales rep for a national supplier. He told me how he'd been requested by the state to submit a bid for some electrical tape. The bids varied from $2,300 to $14,000. His bid was $6,000. He laughed. He had no idea how someone could sell the tape for much less than it cost him. Could they possibly be buying that much better? He could understand someone trying to sell the tape for $14,000, but $2,300? Some people believe that, because the state does a lot of business, they'll sell them the tape and take a loss in hopes of getting other business that will more than make up for that loss. That would be a great strategy except that the state is going to put out bids every time and will always take the lowest one. Packaging only works in the car business, and it doesn't work very well there.

You are selling a service. An older gentlemen gave me this bit of advice my first year in business: "If you're going to go broke, go home and go broke. Don't work hard at it."

Every job must stand on its own. If there ain't profit in it, don't do it.

Chapter 18

IF YOU CAN'T DEBATE IT — THEN YOU MUST BELIEVE IT

Almost everyone would agree that one of the most important ingredients we have to sell is ourselves. Isn't it odd, then, that it's the ingredient we are least prepared to sell? We're far more comfortable bragging about someone else. That needs to change. We must be ready, willing, and able to tell someone why they should buy from us rather than someone else. There are a number of people from whom the prospect can buy similar products. The customer's buying decision then is based not so much on the product as on the salesperson.

You have to be a "persuader" and not a "presenter." If someone asks you why they should buy from you, what will you say? "Because we are the best!" Be careful. Everybody says they're the best; you have to be able to prove it.

Jerry Vass, in his book titled *Soft Selling in a Hard World*, talks about the difference between "proof" statements and "puff" statements. A "puff" statement is made by someone in an attempt to look more favorable in the eyes of another, for example, "We are number one." An example of a "proof" statement is, "We are number one, and let me show you why I can make that statement." Then, of course, proceed to back up the statement with posted statistics, newspaper clippings, testimonials from customers, etc., as proof of that statement. Otherwise, it would just be a "puff" statement.

A kitchen installer in New Jersey tells his prospective clients, "When I started out in business ten years ago, I told everybody I was the best. I figured what the heck, everybody else was saying it. It just so happened for me that it turned out to be true." Isn't that a great line to separate you from the pack?

Whether you have been selling one day or forty-five years, it's time you answered some questions so you will be better prepared on your next sales call. It's important that you write your responses and commit them to memory. One of the objections remodelers hate is when the prospect says, "You are the first person we've talked to, and we need to talk with at least one or two more." Our usual response is, "Mr. and Mrs. Jones, why do you feel the need to do that?" I'll bet this conversation takes place with at least half of the prospects we encounter. Hearing it that often, shouldn't we have a good defense? We should, but most of us don't.

I was on an appointment with a remodeler who was making a very good presentation to a high-tech yuppie and his spouse. The prospect gave the same old "I can't do anything without talking with someone else" line. My guy asked "Why?" The prospect told him, "Because that's what my brother told me to do. He's a builder, and before I started this project I called him and asked him how I should go about doing it. The first thing he said to do was hire an architect, so I hired an architect. He said then contact three reputable contractors and have them bid on the architect's plans. That's exactly what I'm doing now." He added another comment that my contractor friend wasn't prepared for: "If you can give me a good reason why I should not do what my brother suggested, I'll call him tonight and tell him what you said. If he buys into it, we're a done deal." My friend did some stuttering and made a couple of puff statements, but he was unable to offer anything close to a valid reason for the prospect to spend money on a long-distance call to his brother. Since he was not prepared, did that mean he believed the prospect should get three estimates? All these years, we have asked our prospects the "why" question and, as with all good salespeople, we have attempted to counter their response. When the tables are turned and they say "why not?" — we're in trouble.

You must realize that no sales technique works every time on every prospect. The techniques that work best are the ones we believe in. To convince someone we are the best, we must know and believe that. To convince someone our estimate is the only one they need, we must believe that, too. Let's take a closer look at both these issues: (1) Why should someone buy from me? and (2) What does my company offer that distinguishes us from our competition?

While I can't answer those questions for you, I can answer them for me. I tell prospects the reasons they should buy from me are: "Because, first and foremost, I'm honest and, unfortunately, most people in our industry are not. That's why our industry consistently ranks first or second in the annual Better Business Bureau reports in terms of most complaints received. When you buy from me, you can rest assured you will not find your job featured on some news show that's investigating scams. Another reason is that I have a homeowner's mentality not that of a contractor. I think one of the greatest compliments I ever received was just that. A customer once told me, 'The previous contractor we had kept telling us what was industry standard and that it was the best they could do considering what they had to work with. When we complained to you that the work didn't look right, you said you agreed with us and you'd see that it was corrected. You see things through the eyes of the homeowner, and we appreciate that.' What that customer said is true. I don't give a hoot about industry standards. What I care about is trying to obtain the standard of my customers.

"Another real benefit to buying from me is you don't have to worry. You pay me to do the worrying for you. If you are the type of person who is going to worry anyway, I suggest you hire someone else. I assure you that nobody will care more about your project than I do. My record of repeat customers and my customers referring their family members and friends to me speaks for itself. In fifteen years of business, to my knowledge, we have managed to satisfy every one of our customers but one. I ran into one customer who, no matter what we did, we just could not please her. For years, I thought it was all her fault. In retrospect, however, I can see we made our share of mistakes on that job. I'm sorry that my record got tarnished. However, in a business that is so plagued with problems and leaves behind customers saying 'We wouldn't use the same contractor again,' I'm fortunate to have only one. Oh, we run into lots of people who are hard to please, but we just have to work harder to please them. If you are the type of person who cannot be pleased, I would appreciate it if you told me right now. If, however, you can be pleased, let me tell you with complete confidence we can please you."

That was my pitch. I could say that while looking a prospect directly in the eye and without flinching. Remember, the only person we have to sell is often ourselves and, more often than not, there is no one else around to do that for us. It would be nice if we could have a personal-relations person to pitch us, but most of us do not. You have to be ready, willing, and able to brag about yourself. It's easier for some to visualize that they are talking about someone else rather than themselves. Whatever you have to do to blow your own horn, do it. Pull out all the stops, because this may be the only chance you get. Don't blow it.

The next question you need to be prepared to answer is: "What makes your company different?" If I haven't already said so, let me say it now — don't wait on this question or the previous one. If the prospect doesn't ask the question, you ask it yourself by saying, "Mr. Prospect, I'm sure you're asking yourself why you should buy from me or my company. These are good questions. Let me tell you why."

You ask the questions yourself, credit the prospect for asking them, and then proceed to answer them: "Let me tell you what separates us from nearly all other remodeling companies. Number one, we don't start a job until we have the materials. Number two, we don't start a job until we have a crew to do it. Number three, we don't leave a job until we finish it. The biggest complaint we hear from people who have had some remodeling done is that days went by when no one was on the job and the job ran way beyond the scheduled completion date. We work hard to ensure that those things don't happen. Another important factor is that we give you a contract price. If we miscalculated the labor or material, we eat it. Many companies sell using the change order approach — sell at a low price to get the job and then change order the job to death once they get it. This is not to say we don't occasionally have a change order. For example, we could take the

Sheetrock down and discover termites. This is not something anyone could have known until the Sheetrock was removed and, therefore, would require a change order. In our company, these situations are the exception, however, and not the rule. We take great pride in being thorough and trying to complete our jobs without change orders. Often, though, our customers will ask us to do additional work while we are there. We are happy to try and work those changes into our contract and schedule.

"Now, the big question is: Why shouldn't we get more estimates when everything I hear and read says get three estimates? That's a good question, Mr. Jones, and one I'm glad you asked. Unfortunately, our industry is notorious for scams. You have seen them on television, I'm sure. So what else is the media going to say other than, 'Protect yourself, get three estimates'? They can't recommend a specific company to their audiences. I am convinced that people do more harm to themselves than good when they get several estimates. They start off wanting to compare quality, but they get side-tracked by comparing price.

"Ever since people have been studying business economics, they have tried to figure a way, but concluded it impossible, for a company to deliver quality, good service, and lowest price. Notice, Mr. Jones, I did not say *best price*. There is a huge difference between *best* price and *lowest* price. The lowest price always sounds good. Rarely, however, does it deliver the results we want and expect. In fact, Mr. Jones, we surveyed the more than 200 jobs we performed one year and discovered that, if they had been done right the first time by the original remodeling company, 58 percent of the people would not have needed our services. In other words, they paid twice for a job. Many of them thought they were getting the best price. Few actually did. The best price to me is when a product delivers the results I want and expect."

"Mr. Jones, let me get back to the estimates issue. There are approximately 200 contractors in our *Yellow Pages*. Countless others who do so-called 'quality work' are not even listed there. The odds of your getting three reputable contractors are extremely slim. The one who gives you the lowest price is going to make you question the integrity of the others and not the other way around."

Let me share a little story with you. This is perhaps the most extreme example from my years in remodeling, but it is nonetheless a true story. My church referred a woman to me who had just returned from 37 years of missionary work. She'd retired and had inherited an old house that had structural damage. I gave her an approximate price of $10,000 plus any plaster repairs that would be needed on the inside after our underpinning and jacking was done. She didn't give me an answer right then, but agreed to give me one within two days. When I called back, she told me she had received another estimate of $100! What could this lady think except that Phil was ripping her off? I told her, "You certainly don't have to get me to do the work, but please don't pay that other guy $100. All he can possibly do for $100 is go under you house, smoke some cigarettes, come out, and say he's done. Save that $100." I was lucky her son happened to be an engineer. I spent a great deal of time with him on the phone, and we got the job. Certainly, the $100 quote sounded good, but it would have been a total waste of the lady's money. Some say, "What the heck! For $100, I'll take a chance." It's that mentality that will cost you money. Some would even say a price that far off would certainly indicate something is wrong, and they would be right. It's not those ridiculously low bids that get people into trouble as much as it is the job where one contractor priced it at $9,500 and another priced it at $7,500. Most people will assume the quality is the same and that it's the profit margin that's different.

"What I always recommend, Mr. Jones, is to find someone with whom you feel comfortable, someone you can trust, someone who is reputable. Hopefully, you will find that to be us. We are never going to be the cheapest. If we are, I will have made a mistake. In fact, you can talk to any of our past clients and they will tell you that Phil Rea, Inc., is expensive, *but* they are good, that Phil Rea, Inc., is expensive, *but* they do what they said they are going to do. As long as our customers keep calling us back, we are going to keep on doing what we are doing. Mr. Jones, that's a long way to go about telling you that, if you want to get other estimates, okay. But as long as you have my estimate, you don't need to get other estimates."

Be worthy of bragging about yourself…and then do it!

Chapter 19

YOU HAVE THE BEST SALES FORCE A COMPANY COULD EVER WANT — USE IT

We all know the answers to the questions. Here's another one: "Who is the best salesperson a company can possibly have?" A satisfied customer. Even though you already know that, when is the last time you used one of your "salespeople" to help you close a job? Think back for a second to the prospect who asked if they could see some of your work. Whenever someone asks that, you should respond: "I'd love for you to see some of our work. When would you like to do that?" Then set an appointment to pick them up. The key is for you to pick them up at the appointed date and time and for you to take them. Don't tell them you will call some of your customers and find out when is a convenient time. Take care of your prospect first. Later, you can call until you find a couple of previous customers who can meet the appointment time you need.

Those of us who have done this know there is just one problem — we don't do it enough. I can say without reservation that I cannot remember a time when I have taken a prospect to meet a previous customer that I did not get the job. Also, I cannot remember a time when I can honestly say *I* sold it. In each instance, my previous customer "salesperson" sold it. Introduce your prospect and get out of the way. If you need to interject here and there, do so. For the most part, however, let your prospect benefit from the enthusiasm that comes from your previous customer.

If this works so well, why don't we do it more often? We should. This is the highest-percentage close you could possibly have. The reason we don't use it is, quite frankly, because we get lazy, we get out of our game plan, and we don't take the necessary time it takes to be a salesperson. We believe that we can get the end result by taking shortcuts. Make a renewed effort to let your prospects see your sales force face-to-face.

Sometimes prospects will say, often while you are in the close, that they would like to talk with some of your previous customers. Immediately agree, and then ask to use their phone. Keep names and phone numbers in the back of your presentation book for just this purpose. Get one of your previous customers on the phone, preferably one who lives on your prospect's street or in their neighborhood. "Hi, Mrs. Smith, this is Phil Rea. How are you? Mrs. Smith, the reason I'm calling is that I'm down the street from you, and I'm talking with the Joneses about doing some work on their house. They're interested in replacement windows. They aren't familiar with our company and would like to know what kind of a company we are to deal with. Would you be kind enough to talk with Mrs. Jones for just a second? Thank you." After they have their conversation, ask your prospect if Mrs. Smith answered all of the questions. If the answer is "yes," go for the close. If the answer is "no," find out what concerns remain. Try to answer them or get another prospect on the phone if necessary.

Be sure to know what your sales force is going to say. To know that, you need to have someone call any new reference before you let a prospect call them.

I was on an appointment with a remodeler who was on his second call. He was there with the goal of closing the $133,000 job. After his first meeting, he'd given the prospects a sheet of paper with five references, and he'd encouraged them to call them prior to their next meeting. We had not been in the house long when he asked if they had called any of the references. The lady said she had and that one of them was not good. Contractor: "Not good? Did they give a reason?" Prospect: "Yes, she said they were not satisfied." Contractor: "That's strange, we're going to be doing a bath for them in the fall." Prospect: "She said they're going to be doing a bath, but they are not going to be doing it with you." Contractor: "Well, I did deal with her husband primarily. In fact, he asked if we could do the bath when we finished the kitchen but our schedule didn't allow for it." Prospect: "All I can tell you is this lady is not happy."

Now is that the way you want to start an appointment where you have planned to close? First, this person should not have been on the list unless the contractor knew for sure what both the husband and wife were going to say. Second, he should be very grateful that this prospect at least shared the information with him. Although he didn't sell the job, he should have sent her a thank-you card for giving him the information. Third, he should call the previous customer and make an appointment to sit down with them to discuss what had or had not taken place that he needs to know about.

"A professional is one who leaves nothing to chance."

Chapter 20

IT'S ALL IN THE PRESENTATION AND THE PERCEPTION

A few years ago, I bought an old pickup just to haul trash and some light materials for my own personal use. One Friday, I had a lunch meeting scheduled with a friend I had not seen for years. I decided to drive the truck. When he saw me getting out of the pickup, he said, "Phil, one thing I really like about you is your modesty. I'm sure you could afford to drive any car on the market, but you choose to drive an old truck." I was glad when he finally finished, so I could explain to him that it was a vehicle for hauling trash and not what I normally drive. The pickup truck made an impression on him, although it was a false one. This guy assumed more than he should have.

Does the vehicle a person drives tell that much about them? If you think it doesn't, you should read the book *The Millionaire Next Door*. Right or wrong, people draw conclusions.

That truck made a lasting impression on another of my friends. We had decided to go skydiving together. Neither one of us had ever done it before. Even though it was something we wanted to do, we were scared to death to do it. Making the commitment to each other somehow made it easier. I found a place in a nearby town that gave several hours' worth of instruction in the morning and let you make your jump that same afternoon. I told my friend I would pick him up, which I did in my old pickup.

I don't remember him saying much about it at the time, but we have laughed about it a great deal since. He later told me he'd never seen me drive a pickup before. He said he didn't know if I'd driven one this day in case one of us had to come home in a body bag or what, but he did know the pickup didn't ease his anxiety. Again, the pickup made an impression. This friend knew what I normally drove everyday and had never seen this truck before. When he opened his front door and saw a pickup in the driveway, his expectations were not met.

You Can Have Your Cake and Eat It, Too

I was finishing my dessert at a banquet dinner when the lady next to me said, "I'm not sure I can eat my dessert." I was disappointed when she did not go on to say, "Would you like to have it?" Instead she said, "It's too pretty to eat. Did you notice the way the chef did all the different artistic designs with the sauces? He did it on every dessert here. This place has a great dessert chef!" She was into the presentation of the dessert, while I was into eating it. I would not have noticed the designs and probably couldn't have cared less. She was right about the chef though, he took care of both types of customers — those who were into taste and those who were into creativity. People do not like to be surprised when they have expectations. That's as good a way to blow a sale as I know. Do your best to determine what your prospects expect in a remodeler and do all you can to meet those expectations. When you're not sure, do as the chef did: Deliver a good product that both dessert lookers and eaters can appreciate.

Manage the Presentation

I went on a call with a salesperson. He pulled out the proposal and handed it to the prospect. He said he believed everything was in there that they had discussed. I was shocked. I don't know what the prospect expected, but it couldn't have been what he was getting. I wondered what the salesperson's expectations were as well. He had told me on the way to the appointment that the goal was to get a signature. Instead of selling, he just gave the guy a three-page typewritten proposal. The prospect did the same thing any of us would probably have done. He said, "I'll look it over and get back with you."

When someone gives you a book, do you sit down and start reading it right then? I don't think so. My sales rep started putting some closes on the poor guy. He knew he was supposed to close, but he did not know how to present. He did not know that, once someone is sold, price is no longer the issue. He should have brought out a copy of the proposal for each person involved and then started reading it aloud himself. After reading each item, he should have asked, "Is that what you wanted Mr. Smith?" Or, "Do you have any questions about that?" Or, "Are we clear about that? Did I miss anything?"

When you get to the end of a presentation, you want to make certain all the questions are answered. Only then is it time to pull out the contract. It really amazes me that we are able to sell as much product as we do. It just shows what a high demand there is for our services. When times get tight, however, you'd better know how to do it right.

He Was Selling Air...and I Bought

The way to do it right is the way a radio advertising salesperson did it. I had never even considered advertising on the radio, much less requested to have a salesperson call on me. However, one dropped by to see me one afternoon. I figured he was just trying to fill his quota for cold calls. But this was a far cry from any other "drop in" I'd ever experienced. This guy had two commercials that were already made up and customized for me. They were good ads! He must have gone to some trouble to not only write them, but have someone cut them. When he asked, "Which one do you like the best?" I had a hard time deciding. I liked them both. They not only appealed to my ego, they had the potential to enhance my business. I went from having no interest in radio advertising to signing a contract for six weeks of air time.

Previously, when someone would call me about radio, television, or even newspaper advertising, I would ask them why I should buy advertising from them when it was all I could do to service the prospects I had. If they could convince me that I should, then I would consider their proposals. This guy was a salesperson who recognized the importance of making a presentation. If he had called for an appointment, he would have been given that same line. Instead, he chose to invest in my business. His presentation far exceeded my expectations.

Make certain your presentations exceed the expectations of your prospects!

Chapter 21

WHEN YOU NEED HELP, GET IT ... THEN KEEP IT

My remodeling business was growing by leaps and bounds. Heck, I'm a compulsive salesperson. I couldn't have stopped the growth even if I knew how. When I finally realized the business was getting away from me, I called in a consultant. I'll never forget the fact that I paid this guy a lot of money to tell me I needed to hire three more people in the office. That was not the answer I was looking for. Throw money at the problem? Not me! I hired one new person. My answer was to do more and to expect more out of my people. There is certainly nothing wrong with expecting 100 percent from yourself and your people, but recognize that is the maximum you can get.

I ended up pushing myself to the point where I completely burned out. I was working as many hours as possible. And, when I was not working, I was worrying. One day, I decided I'd had enough and that I needed a sabbatical. For four months, I did not go into the office or call in. To my dismay, the company made money. I discovered that the people I'd hired were actually quite capable of doing their jobs. I returned to work not only rested, but resolved to delegate. I quit working nights and weekends. I didn't take work home, and I continued taking most of the summers off. You probably won't believe this, because I certainly wouldn't have, but my profits increased. I worked less and made more money.

You can, too. Analyze what you are doing that someone else could do more efficiently. If you are a good salesperson, spend your time selling. If you are good at swinging the hammer and that's your passion, then find a salesperson. When you get too busy to do it all, don't do it. Contrary to what you may believe, there are highly qualified people who are looking for a good place to work. It is getting harder and harder, however, to find these people. I agree with others in our industry when they say that those who control the labor will control the market. In other words, if you can't produce it, what good will it do you to sell it? The good full-service remodeling salespeople in this industry have little trouble outselling their labor forces ten months out of the year. Attracting quality people certainly has the potential to increase your bottom line because they enable you to sell and produce more work. It is even more important to retain the quality people who are currently under your employ.

A company owner told me he wasn't going to pay a guy $15 an hour *and* give him two breaks a day. I asked if the guy was a good worker. He told me he wouldn't be there if he weren't. I asked him how much backlog he currently had, and he said he'd been turning down work for months. I told him that if I were in his position, I would pay that guy $25 an hour if I had to. He wouldn't be paying him, his customers who want him to do their work would be paying him. Then, if the well dried up and I didn't have any work, I would let him go.

In my business, I had no choice. I personally did not have the skills to build a room addition or install replacement windows or remodel a kitchen. I recognized how important my labor force was, and I made every effort to show my appreciation for them. That included offering a fair and reasonable wage. If a person is entitled to a raise, doggone it, give it to them and don't make them beg for it. You never want to lose a good employee to a competitor who's willing to pay higher wages when you are willing to pay higher wages yourself.

Also, take a percentage of your profits and start a retirement account. Every year when we funded our account, we made a big deal of it. We had the employees and the spouses attend our annual profit-sharing dinner at a local restaurant. The company that handled our pension fund had a folder on everyone that informed them what their share of the year's funding was and showed them the history of their account. This was a great loyalty-building outing. The key was involving the spouses. I knew at some point the spouse who worked for me would get fed up and want to quit. I wanted the other spouse armed with all the ammunition I could give them so they would convince them to stay. It was for that reason we did picnics, cruises, local trips, and even a trip to Hawaii.

If you need help, get it by hiring additional staff. There is an old saying, "You can throw an old dog a bone." That simply means that you shouldn't take for granted those folks who have been working with you, they may one day take up the steak that someone else is prepared to give.

If you don't treat your employees right, they will one day accept the better offer your competitor is willing to give them.

Chapter 22

ENTER A CONTEST EVERY MONTH — YOURS

We had a basketball hoop outside our house. Each night when I came home, I used to try to make ten baskets from the free-throw line before I would allow myself to go inside. My basketball abilities were improving, but my wife would occasionally have to tell me to come in. I would try and do the same type of disciplined and competitive thing in sales each month. I would count the number of workdays, set my gross profit goal (I don't care about volume, it's the profit I like), and establish a reward system. Some months it might be a round of golf, other months it might be a long weekend at a nice resort. We all work to pay the bills, put the kids through college, and have something left over for retirement, but sometimes we need more than that. We need a reward system that enables us to pat ourselves on the back.

I always like to get the first quarter of the year off to a good start by having a contest for the salespeople. Typically, I would go to my window and siding supplier, and I'd ask how many windows and how many squares of siding we would have to sell in three months to get him to pay for all of us and our spouses to have an evening on the town. (My supplier will verify we always won the contest.) It wasn't that we were not capable of selling that amount on our own, it was just so much more fun and challenging to set up a contest for ourselves.

If you are the only salesperson, establish a contest for yourself, one that exceeds what you would normally do, one that is going to make you work smarter. One of our salespeople specialized in room additions. I was amazed at how many window jobs he sold with those additions when the contest was going on. When the contest was over, his window sales dropped off drastically.

You would think that the profit from the sales would be motivation enough, but often it isn't. I have worked harder for a "Sales Rep of the Month" plaque than I have ever worked for a $1,000 commission.

If you have a sales force, you can increase production by 10 to 20 percent just with contests. Make them not only profitable, but fun. An old "steak and beans" contest (where you divide your people up into two teams and the winners eat steak and the losers sit on the other side of the table eating their beans) works as well today as it did 20 years ago.

People still love winning and hate losing. That will never change.

Chapter 23

EVERYBODY NEEDS A COACH

Johnny's mother went though the same routine almost every morning. She would get up, start breakfast, and go to the bottom of the stairs and holler, "Johnny, time to get up, get dressed for school, and come down for breakfast." She knew from experience it normally took about three of these trips to the steps before Johnny muttered a word. Johnny's response was typically, "Momma, give me one reason why I should get out of this bed." Momma replied, "I'm going to give you two. One, you're forty-four years old. Two, you are the school principal. Get down here!"

No matter how high up the ladder you go, you still need a coach. Tiger Woods, arguably one of the greatest golfers in history, has several coaches. The Chicago Bulls, the premier basketball team of the 1990s, has twelve players and five coaches. You don't need one, right? We all need to spend time with someone who sees more in us than we see in ourselves. For many, that coach is a parent. For others, it might be a friend or a professional acquaintance. The coach has to be someone who motivates *and* holds you accountable for the results you want to produce.

We have a theme park in our area that has one of the fastest and highest roller coasters in the country. When I took my daughter to the park, she wouldn't ride it with me. I was relieved. Still, it kept nagging at me. I was scared, yet I wanted to experience the excitement. I needed a coach, so I called a neighbor who had a season pass to the park and said, "Let's go ride Alpengeist after work today." He became my coach and didn't know it. You can all do as I did and choose a coach for yourself.

I worked on this book for several years. It only took about sixty days of work, but it actually took three years because I was always thinking of all the things I could be doing instead. The book was important to me. Not only did I have something I wanted to say, but it would mean increased demand and credibility for my speaking business which, in turn, would mean more money. You would think I had more than sufficient incentive, wouldn't you? I had the incentive, but I needed a coach to help provide the motivation.

That coach presented herself. No, it wasn't my wife who kept telling me not to take on another job until I had finished the book. It wasn't even several of my friends who would periodically inquire how the book was coming. I certainly appreciated their interest and sometimes it even provided the inspiration to write a page or two. My coach arrived in the form of a postcard from California.

The person who sent the card had sat next to me for a session at a writers' conference. We talked at a break for maybe fifteen minutes. I thought she was a nice person and had enjoyed our conversation, but I didn't remember giving her my business card. This was not a relationship I planned to nourish; it was just one of those pleasant encounters with a person that occur each day in the gym, at the store, or a social outing. Her card arrived on May 28. In it, she challenged me to finish the book and said she would write again in a few weeks to check on my progress. Her challenge became the inspiration I needed. Don't misunderstand me, this is not just any person who might have walked in off the street without a clue of what it takes to do a book. She has done several herself and was, therefore, qualified to be a writer's coach. I'm certain she knew that, by simply writing a postcard, she would have a powerful impact on me. How was this possible? How was it that someone I didn't know could get me moving on a project about which I'd been so complacent for so long?

We all need coaches in our lives, those special individuals who come alongside us because they see something in us that, for whatever reasons, we resist seeing in ourselves. My new-found coach even addressed her card to: "Phil Rea, Author." No one had ever called me that before.

Be on the lookout for the person who crosses your path who can help you be all you want to be. And be on the lookout for those you can coach as well.

Chapter 24

GET GOOD AT SELLING THE APPOINTMENT

There is much more to selling than just selling your product or services. You often have to take steps to put yourself in position to make the sale. Football teams put themselves in position to score points far more frequently than mistakes by opposing teams put them in that position. Before you can sell your product, you must become effective at selling the appointment.

It is extremely important that all parties who will be involved in the purchasing decision be there for your presentation. In today's society, this could be the most difficult part of your sell. What typically happens is the wife starts suggesting to the husband some improvement she would like to have done. The husband finally says either, "Get some prices, and let me know what you find out," or "Just do it." You and I both know that, at some point, the non-participating spouse will usually enter the picture. How well you do at getting them involved from the very beginning will have a huge influence on your success in making the sale.

I worked with a new salesperson, Sally, who was having trouble getting both spouses together for the initial appointment. I sat down with her to observe her technique. The first lead Sally called was very typical. The wife had called Sally's firm to schedule an appointment to discuss a room addition.

Remodeling salespeople of America: How many of you, for one second, think a married person, male or female, is going to make a decision as important as buying a room addition without involving their spouse? Perhaps some of you can think of one or two jobs you sold and never met the spouse, but how many more appointments have you gone on when the spouse wasn't there and you were told, "Everything sounds real good to me. Let me talk with my spouse, and I'll get back with you." You are still waiting to hear from most of those.

You may have done a good job of selling one spouse, but that spouse may not be as good a salesperson in selling their partner as you were in selling them. If they were, you would have heard from them. Who is the salesperson here? You! You should be the one doing the selling. I would occasionally get a prospect who needed to talk with a relative or another advisor. I would say, "Mr. Jones, I'm sure they are going to have numerous questions. Let's get them on the phone right now." My reason? I'm the best person here to do the selling.

Let's get back to the appointment-setting I was doing with Sally. When she asked the prospect when would be a good time to get together with her and her husband, she was informed that Bill was going to have nothing to do with this project and that the entire decision rested solely on her. Sally talked briefly over the phone about the scope of the project, and the homeowner asked her to give a rough ballpark price based upon their discussion. Sally answered that it would be roughly $100,000 to $130,000. She ended up making an appointment for the next afternoon, and I accompanied her.

Sally really did a great job warming up. She made a very good presentation of the company and of herself. Everything was going along extremely well. Hers was a design/build firm that asks for a deposit on the initial appointment. In return for this deposit, the client is given a price to do the project based on hours of work instead of grabbing a number out of the air. This deposit rarely, if ever, covered the amount of time invested, it simply separated the buyers from the shoppers. The deposit is also applied to the project if they decide to proceed. The deposit for this project, based on its size, was to be $1,000. Prior to asking for the deposit, Sally asked the homeowner if she was comfortable with everything. "Oh, yes. Everything sounds good to me." But right on cue, when Sally asked for the money, the lady said, "I couldn't give you any deposit without talking to Bill." What in the world happened? Yesterday, this same person had total responsibility for this project, and, today, she can't make a $1,000 decision? Again, you and I know this is not the exception, it's the norm. It's that way in my house. Neither I nor my wife is going to make that kind of decision without the other. How could I expect someone else to?

My question to you is, "Why do you keep going? Why do you continue to put yourself in non-selling situations? Is your time of no value to you?" Perhaps it is not politically correct to insist that both parties be present. Be aware you can go dead broke being politically correct. Concentrate on selling, and let the politicians worry about being politically correct.

When the prospect calls you for the appointment, be proactive. Stop kidding yourself that, when they tell you they don't need the other spouse, this one will be different. You don't have the time to take that chance. Your job is to sell something today. The odds of a sale happening on a "one-legger" (an appointment where only one spouse is present) are not good. If this were a poker game, you would fold that hand. Instead of waiting for the prospect to tell you they don't need their spouse, you tell them *you* need their spouse. "Mrs. Jones, when is a good time to get together with you and Mr. Jones? — and let me tell you why I ask that. I would be saying the same thing to him had he called for the appointment instead of you. I will have questions for you, I promise you, that he will not be able to answer. I also promise you I will have questions for him that you will not be able to answer. In an effort to provide you with the information you both will require to make an informed decision, I will need you both there. I can come one morning, before he goes to work, or perhaps he can come home early one afternoon. What time will suit you better?" If the party insists on meeting you alone, I'm not going to say, "Don't go." Go if you must, but go knowing you did not sell the appointment, and before you can sell the job, you are going to need to bring the other party into the picture.

Many salespeople will refuse to go if both spouses are not present. If they get there and one of them is missing, they leave. These are the same salespeople, for the most part, who give the prospect one opportunity to buy. Perhaps this is not your style.

Frankly, it's not mine either. Don't for one second think, however, that their style is not effective. This style is used by the "tin men" of our industry.

It is hard even today, in the politically correct world in which we live, to find a salesperson who outsells a good "tin man."

Chapter 25

TAKE ENTHUSIASM ON EVERY SALES CALL

Did you know that the salesperson's enthusiasm is frequently the deciding factor in whether or not a prospect buys? Enthusiasm is a huge factor, but it's not the only factor.

When I started in the home-improvement business, I was not prepared for a period of training. I had been selling cars and was good at it. I didn't need any training. I thought I would just start knocking doors my first day and keep knocking them until I made an appointment and then I would call in for an experienced person to take over from there. When the owner of the company said he wanted to spend a week training me, I was shocked. This job was 100 percent commission. I knew darn well I wasn't going to sit in a class for a week. I persuaded the owner to give me a couple hours of training on one of their many products so I could specialize until I acquired the necessary knowledge to sell others. He agreed and thought the easiest and most profitable product for me to concentrate on would be their blown-in insulation.

By the afternoon of my first day, I was out knocking doors. My friend, who had introduced me to the business, was on one side of the street, and I was on the other. I was elated when I knocked on Mrs. Carter's door and she consented to an appointment later that evening. She said this would give her husband the opportunity to eat supper and relax a few minutes after coming in from work. My friend said he would make the presentation for me so I could see a "spread" from start to finish. I would have nothing to do with that. This was *my* appointment. I could handle it. He was welcome, however, to come along and watch me sell it.

I was an experienced sales professional, so I had no problem with the approach or the warm-up and was full of enthusiasm going into the presentation. The company had a standard pitch book, so all that really was involved was reading the captions over the pictures. No problem there. Then, I got to the point in the presentation book where it called for removing an outlet cover and putting a screwdriver outside the box to determine if there was any insulation in the walls. I was supposed to be able to determine his savings based on what insulation he presently had. I had my screwdriver with me and removed the outlet. My enthusiasm surpassed my knowledge when I turned to the prospect and said, "Mr. Carter, no wonder your utility bills are so high. You don't have a bit of insulation in those walls." He said, "I'm not supposed to have any insulation in an interior wall." I was checking the wall separating the den from the dining room. My friend was laughing so hard he almost fell off the sofa.

No, I didn't sell that job. I didn't have a clue as to how to recover. But, by the end of my first month, I was the company's number one salesperson out of eight. I gradually accumulated a little knowledge to go with my enthusiasm. Most salespeople feel as though they have to have all the information before they can leave the office. You can never know everything. You just need to know where you can find the answers.

Yes, you need to know your products. More importantly, you need enthusiasm for your products and your company. When it comes down to it, your enthusiasm will sell more jobs than product knowledge will.

"Knowledge instills confidence, confidence instills enthusiasm, and enthusiasm sells."

Chapter 26

VISUALIZATION

Most people are visual. They take what you say and turn it into mental pictures. Good salespeople know this and paint these pictures for them. This is another reason for having a good pictorial presentation book and using it on every sales call. You don't just talk to prospects about buying a deck. Instead, you should say something like, "I can certainly see why you would want a deck here. Sitting out here with that morning cup of coffee, admiring the beauty of your backyard appears to me like a great way to start a day." Or, "When you add this new family room, you're going to wonder how in the world you ever lived in this house without it. This will be where you will want to spend your time. Have you visualized where the TV will be?" Or, if you're selling siding, "Mr. Jones, what are you going to do with all the free time you're going to have this summer since your not going to be painting the house? I'm sure a fishing pole or a golf club in the hand will feel much better than a paintbrush."

Napoleon Hill, the author of *Think and Grow Rich*, said, "If you can conceive it and believe it, you can achieve it." It begins with conceive, which means to create a mental image. When you go on a sales call, do you see yourself sitting at the kitchen table with the homeowners signing the contract? You should. What would you have to see taking place in order for the contract signing to occur? Learn to utilize the power of visualization.

A college basketball player, whose team recently won the national championship, was interviewed after the game. He was asked if he ever imagined anything like this happening to him. He said he had been to a championship game as an eight-year-old boy and, from that point on, had not only seen himself in the championship game, but being the hero of the winning team. He wasn't surprised. He had visualized that day for years.

I was told the story of a gentleman who really enjoyed playing golf. As is the case with a lot of us, his enjoyment wasn't directly related to his ability to play the game. Due to circumstances beyond his control, he went nearly 17 years without playing. Without ever picking up a club during that time, he improved his score from 94 to 74. How is that possible? Visualization. You see, this gentleman was a prisoner of war in Vietnam and, to occupy his mind each day, he played a mental game of golf. He visualized his attire, the weather conditions of the day, what he thought about as he walked to his ball in anticipation of his next shot, etc. After his release, he returned to the course where he'd shot a 94 on his last golf outing. He shot a 74.

Golf is visual, but it's no more visual than selling. Justin Leonard, who won the 1997 British Open at twenty-five years of age, marks his ball on the green with a coin that was minted in the 1960s. This serves as a constant visual reminder that he wants to score in the sixties every round of golf he plays.

Come up with something that works for you, just as the coin does for Leonard. For me, I always counted the number of days I was going to work each month and determined how many jobs I was going to sell. I would get my sales record form and put that many blanks on it. Then it was just a matter of filling in those blanks with a name. I kept this form in my appointment book so I couldn't help but see it throughout the day.

Don't just show up on appointments and see what happens — visualize what you want to happen.

Chapter 27

TO MAKE MONEY, YOU MUST SELL MONEY

I was on an appointment recently with a salesperson who was told by the prospect that his price was $500 higher than that of the competition. Without hesitation, however, the prospect said, "If I can put the work on my VISA, you can have the job." He didn't ask, "Can you reduce the price?" Or, "What are you doing for that $500 that the other company is not doing?"

This is not unusual. People want convenience, and easy-payment terms make things convenient. A large percentage of people are payment buyers. You need to sell the way they buy. Look at the building suppliers' advertisements in your paper. They are not selling kitchens — they are selling easy, affordable monthly payments in order to have a new kitchen. Here are just a few of the many reasons you should be offering financing to your prospects:

1. *You control the deal.* Your prospects need to obtain the money from someplace, so why shouldn't it be you? You work hard to sell the job only to have the prospect go to their local banker, and the banker says something to mess up the deal for you. Very rarely will someone ask if you offer financing. They assume you do not. Therefore, they think it is their job to get a price from you and then seek out the funding elsewhere. You make it much more attractive when your prospect is able to deal with just one person — you!

2. *Financing can turn tomorrow's job into today's work.* Financing has sold a number of jobs for me over the years. One that particularly stands out was a job my draftsman and I were on. We were standing in the prospect's backyard discussing the project, when she abruptly said, "Phil, now I told your secretary that I was not going to be able to do this project till eighteen months from now." I asked her why. She said she was going to be getting the money from the sale of some farmland and that is when she would have the money. I immediately knew that financing gave me several alternatives that would possibly allow me to overcome that objection. This, however, was not the time to exercise them. I needed to sell her on the project first. This is where many salespeople make a mistake by getting ahead of themselves. It would be pretty foolish of me to sell financing before selling her on the project. My draftsman did a beautiful design and drawing, and she fell in love with the project. She closed herself by saying, "How soon could you start? I'm going to sell some stock to pay for this, and I'll just reimburse myself when I get the farm money." I did not get the opportunity to use any of my closes. I didn't sell that job with financing. But, if I hadn't had a financing plan in my bag of sales tools, I probably would not have gotten the job.

3. ***Payments don't make the price less, but they sure make it sound like a lot less.*** You tell me which sounds better: "Mr. and Mrs. Jones, we can do the entire job we talked about today for $26,854." Or, "We can do everything we talked about for $251 per month." I'm not trying to hide the price of the job, but I am trying to make it sound more attractive. Never mind what the total price will be with interest. In most cases, you can write off a large portion of that anyhow. When someone buys a house, do they figure up how much the house is going to cost over the life of the mortgage? I think not. Most buy the payment knowing that they are not going to be there for thirty years. People buy remodeling the same way.

Let's break this cost down even further. Let's say you have the $26,000 job and you have a payment of $251. Your prospect keeps referring to how much money $26,000 is. You handle the prospect by finding out how long they are going to be living in that house. Let's say it's five years. In five years, they would pay $251 a month for sixty months for a total of $15,060.

Now ask them how much they think this improvement will add to the value of their house in five years, taking into consideration inflation and increased real-estate value. (*Remodeling Magazine* does a cost-versus-value report each year that can be a great sales aid.) Let's just say they think the improvement will increase the value of their home by $20,000 in five years. I would then show them how the interest could be set up as a tax deduction. Let's assume that $8,000 of that $15,000 goes for interest. He has an interest deduction of $8,000 and the property value increased by $20,000. Here's the closing line: "Mr. and Mrs. Jones, not only are you going to have the enjoyment of the new space, but it appears to be a good financial investment as well. Don't you agree?" This is not at all complicated, it just sounds complicated at first. If you can figure out how much load a beam will carry, this will be elementary for you.

4. ***Selling financing can turn a "no" into a "yes."*** When qualifying one of my prospects I asked her, "In terms of a monthly payment, how much do you want to invest in your siding project?" She responded, "I will be paying cash." When I gave her the price of $13,500, she informed me that she had a price of $12,000 from another company and they were using the same product. They had done the house across the street and the work looked good to her. She added, "I'm not going to pay you $1,500 more, because I'm saving to have the kitchen done." Without hesitation, I told her the advantages of keeping her money in the bank and financing both the siding *and* the kitchen. I left there that day with a contract for both jobs without another word being said about being what she perceived as $1,500 higher on the siding.

Here is an example of how you sell a person who has the money in the bank: "Mr. and Mrs. Jones, have you even considered letting the bank pay for your job? I think you will agree it's easier to take the money out of the bank than it is to put it in. Many of our customers have been able to get the best from both worlds. This job is $26,854. In most accounts today, that amount will yield about 8 percent interest, or about $2,200 per year. Your payment is only going to be approximately $3,000 per year, and you can deduct the interest from your taxes (second mortgage loans). If you have some of those high return years, such as we've had recently, you could yield much more than the 8 percent. Also, consider that, if you keep the loan the full term, when it is paid off, the $26,854 you had in the bank is now worth approximately $90,000."

5. ***Folks will pay you more, because they have more.*** As I pointed out in the last example, a cash customer only has so much cash. If they plan to pay cash, the scope of the work is limited by the amount of cash they have — not so with the finance buyer. A prospect who only has $30,000 cash to invest in a project that you figure is going to cost $37,000 has options with financing. They can finance the entire package or pay the $30,000 down and finance the $7,000.

6. ***Change orders are not a problem when you know where to get the money.*** In reviewing a company's delinquent account receivables recently, almost every question I asked was answered with, "The job kept growing and, at the end, the money was not there." Financing could have alleviated that problem. When I call in a job to the bank, I often call it in for more money than what I need so I won't be concerned about add-ons. I know if I'm doing siding and I want to sell them windows, the money is available and it's only a matter of selling a $20 or $30 payment. In most cases, the windows will pay that in terms of energy savings.

7. ***Selling on payments can eliminate your competition, and they won't know it until it's over.*** I once asked a couple, "In terms of monthly payment, how much do you want to invest in this bathroom?" They proceeded to tell me they'd had a bankruptcy and did not know how much money they could get. They did know that water was leaking into their dining room and they needed to do something as soon as possible. I told them the best way to handle this was to take a credit application and see how much money the lenders would give them and then go from there. We were able to obtain a loan for $5,800. This did not do a

complete make-over, but it did allow us to do the necessary items. While we were there working, one of our competitors, who had talked with the folks previously, drove up with plans in hand in anticipation of making a fancy presentation to the people. I actually felt sorry for him, knowing he had invested that much time without knowing what he was investing in.

8. *Selling financing just increased your number of potential prospects.* Not everybody has money, and not everybody can borrow money. But the number of people who can borrow is far greater than the number who have it. One of the primary lenders I used would lend $50,000 based on no equity. That's right. The prospect could move into the house today with no equity and get up to $50,000 in improvements tomorrow. I can do a lot of improvements for $50,000.

Can you imagine a carpenter not having a hammer? That's what the salesperson is without financing. Carpenters don't use their hammers everyday. Some days, they may be finishing Sheetrock or another type of job that doesn't require a hammer. But, when they need those hammers, they need those hammers. You may not always need financing. You may say that you have been going all these years and survived very nicely without it. Well, your ancestors got along fine without cars, televisions, or computers — what does that have to do with you?

Any remodeler who does residential remodeling and does not provide a method of payment for those prospects is making a costly mistake.

Chapter 28

TWO WORDS THAT WILL MAKE YOU MONEY: "I'M SORRY"

You would think that some things are so basic that they wouldn't need to be discussed. However, that is not the case. The great football coach Vince Lombardi started the first practice of every pre-season holding up a football and saying, "Gentlemen, this is a football." Certainly the professional football players under Coach Lombardi knew what a football was. That was about as basic as it can get. Basics, however, were not something he took for granted. "I'm sorry" should not to be taken for granted either.

As I sit and pen these words, I'm in the Los Angeles Airport. I just returned my rental car. I had contracted for a mid-size car for the week, but, when I went to pick up my car, they did not have a mid-size. I agreed to accept a compact at a lower cost. I was told they would adjust the price when I returned the car. When I turned the car in, however, I was told I owed more. I told the woman I had been quoted less for the mid-size than what she was now trying to charge me for the smaller car. She said that had been without all the insurance options. I had not agreed to any insurance options. In fact, I had declined them, and my initials on my contract showed that. She said, "It's in the system that you accepted the insurance. Anyone could have initialed the contract." She seemed to be implying that I was a dishonest cheapskate. Reluctantly, she agreed to call the location where I had picked up the car to see if they could straighten things out. When she hung up, I asked if she had it all taken care of. She simply said, "Yes." I had been standing at the counter for thirty minutes. That's all I was going to get? I don't think so. "What was the problem?" I asked. As it turned out, I had been correct. She had made a mistake, not the people at the pick up location. She had incorrectly entered the data into the computer herself.

I am certainly sympathetic to people making mistakes. The entire matter could have been resolved by her saying, "I'm sorry." Or, "My fault, I'm sorry." Or, "I'm so sorry, I made a mistake." But she didn't say anything, and that irritated me more than the problem had.

Why is it so hard for people to say "I'm sorry" today? It seems everyone has to justify being right. I once had a client who had a four-page punch list that he and his wife both wanted to personally present to me. When I arrived at their home I said, "I will sit here and listen as long as you want to talk, but do you mind if I say a couple things first?" They both agreed. I went on to say, "When I sold you this remodeling, I told you it would disrupt your lifestyle, but I never intended for it to be as disruptive as it has been and for that I'm sorry. I also told you that we would communicate with you all along the way. You would not have to inquire when the wallpaper hanger would be here or when your fixtures would be installed. I said our company would provide you with that information beforehand. That communication did not take place, and I'm sorry. You invested a great deal of trust, confidence, and money with me, and I'm sorry that I let you down." The husband stood, tore up the punch list, and said, "There are just a couple of little things I'd like for you to take care of." I encountered a very unhappy client, but I left one who said that, if I ever needed to use them as a reference, I should feel free to do so. I could have easily tried to turn it around and make them feel that the project had not met either of our expectations and much of the blame should be borne by them. I could have reminded them that the wallpaper they picked out had been discontinued, but they wanted us to try and get it anyway. There were numerous things that occurred during the project that were their fault. Equally as many were my fault, and those were the only ones they wanted to talk about. Since I wasn't excited about going over each and every one of the items the four pages contained, I just gave a big old "I'm sorry." This customer owed me a great deal of money, and I learned a very valuable lesson. Treat every customer as if they owe you $50,000. Not only will you leave with your check, but you will most likely create a satisfied customer.

The lady at the car-rental agency could have changed my attitude and sent me away smiling even after all the hassle simply by saying, "I'm sorry." Why didn't she? If she thought she didn't have enough to invest to make me happy, she was wrong. She most likely cost the company a client.

"I'm sorry" are two words you should love to say. They don't cost you a cent and could make you lots of money. They will also make you stand out because so few people are able to say them.

Chapter 29

YOU NEVER WANT TO GRADUATE FROM "SELLING 101"

A few months ago, I had the pleasure of working with a remodeling salesperson during his first two days on the job. The company had grown to a point where the owner needed a sales rep to carry some of the load. After many interviews, he decided to give a young man in his organization a chance. This guy had been with the company for some time and was the highest-producing carpenter in the company. I agreed with the owner that finding a new carpenter would be much easier than finding a good salesperson. He asked if I would spend some time with his new salesperson in hopes of getting him started on the right foot. I agreed that laying a good foundation and instilling the proper work ethic were critical.

There is great truth in the saying: "Give a man a fish and he can eat for days — but, if you teach him to fish, he can eat for life."

Even though the owner had more leads than he could effectively handle, there was no guarantee that this would always be the case. It was important for me to teach this guy to prospect not only for the owner's sake, but for his. The weather that first day was ugly. We knocked doors in snow, sleet, rain, and ice. I taught him how to take good notes about the house when the homeowner was not there. These notes would be extremely helpful when he called on them again. We needed to be able to personalize the call instead of sounding like the typical phone solicitor.

We made five appointments for the next day. That first evening, we went back to the office so I could show him the skills involved in making effective phone calls. When I said, "Okay, now it's your turn," he did something I had never seen done before.

His first three calls resulted in three appointments. Now, that's like a rookie being called up to the major leagues and, in his first three at-bats, hitting three home runs against Nolan Ryan. This guy was a natural. He had the nerve, the poise, the confidence, and the expertise of a seasoned professional. His first two weeks, he sold five jobs. That's right, a raw rookie sold five jobs. That's not all. These jobs were not friends or relatives or even good leads the owner had given him. These were "teach me to fish" leads. Three had come as a result of his knocking on doors. The other two were leads the owner was going to discard because the prospects were going to get three estimates. With his workload, that's the last thing he wanted. The rookie took those two leads and turned them both into sales. So much for their getting three estimates. I was so proud of this guy I didn't know what to do!

The owner and I decided I should visit with the salesperson again in ninety days. We recognized the potential for some bad habits to sneak up on his prized find, and we wanted to keep that from happening. When I arrived on my second visit, I jumped right in the truck with the sales rep. He had scheduled several appointments for the day, and there was no time to waste. On the drive to the first appointment, he told me this one was not going to be good because they did not live in a good area, they didn't have any money, and it was going to be a "one-legger." I told him to stop the truck. I wanted to know where he learned all of these fortune-telling techniques. It's not what I taught him three months ago. This was exactly why I was there, to keep work habits like these from happening. I was shocked that they already had. As good as he'd been early on, the sophomore jinx had hit him early and hit him hard. This happens to most salespeople. The ones who have successful careers are the ones who can come out of it. The ones who are good at practicing the K.I.S.S. (Keep It Simple, Stupid) principle. They don't try to prove to everyone how smart they are like my man was doing. He was a mind reader, a fortune teller, and a banker all rolled into one. As it turned out, he was wrong on all counts. The people had a nice house, both spouses were present, and they had the cash to make the purchase. He was too shocked to sell them. Eventually, he got his act together and had a tremendous rookie year.

Selling is something you have to do over and over each and every day, using the same formula that made you successful the day before. You don't need to invent a new way to sell. You just need to use the ones you already know. Michael Jordan is great. But, because he scored 30 points last night, what does that have to do with him scoring 30 points tonight? Is there any guarantee he can do it again? Is he going to invent any new shots overnight? He has to do just what you have to do — stick with the basics, go with what got you there. Like Michael Jordan, you might have a bad game or two, but that does not mean you need to reinvent your game? You keep taking it to the hoop, keep presenting your product, keep going for the close.

If you've taken "Selling 101," that means you know the basics. The only advancement you want is to become wiser and more experienced. Trust me, you don't need any advanced courses.

Chapter 30

THE FULL ROUTINE

My children and I got into an argument one night about whether their mother, my wife, cooked chicken six or seven nights out of seven. Thank goodness, we all love chicken. I've said that, if they find out chicken will kill you, I'm going to kill myself. Many nights, we would watch her put the chicken in the oven, and we would all quietly pray that lasagna or a meatloaf would come out. It never happened. Chicken in, chicken out.

The same might be said of your recipe for selling. If it is not producing a sale on one-third to one-half of all the presentations you make, you need to take a look at your recipe. "If you always do what you've always done, you'll always get what you always got."

I want to share with you the recipe that I have used to sell lots of jobs and make lots of money. I use it on every sales call. It is extremely rare that I do not use it in the exact order that I'm going to show you. I encourage you to use it, too. It works for me and it will work for you as well. If you have a good selling recipe now, stick with it, don't change. If you're not satisfied with your results, however, this is a great recipe to have.

THE FULL ROUTINE
APPROACH
WARM-UP
QUALIFYING
PRESENTATION
CLOSE
FOLLOW-UP

1. **Approach:** *Your goal in the approach is to show your prospects how professional you are.*

When the phone rang at your office, the approach began. The prospects formed their first impression of your company. Now, you are going to their house where they will form their first impression of you. What better way to make a favorable impression than to be on time for the appointment? Very few professionals show regard for the customer's time these days. You score huge points when you arrive on schedule. If you are going to be more than five minutes late, call the prospects to let them know. There aren't many good excuses for being late, so don't offer one — just apologize. I run very few evening appointments and rarely a weekend appointment. Therefore, in most cases, the prospects have come home from work to meet with me. It is especially important that their time be respected.

Whenever possible, arrive in the neighborhood fifteen minutes prior to your appointment. This allows you a little leeway. More important, it allows you the chance to ride through and see the neighborhood. During sales calls, the "move versus improve" question frequently arises. This extra time should help prepare you to discuss the benefits of staying put and remodeling.

Park your car properly on the street. Don't walk on the lawns. Pick up the newspaper. You might be surprised to know how many people observe your behavior as you approach their house. I like to ring the doorbell at exactly the time of my appointment. I say, "Mr. Prospect, I'm Phil Rea. I had a two o'clock appointment with you and Mrs. Prospect." Almost without exception, they look at their watches and make a comment about my punctuality. I typically respond by saying, "I know your time is valuable. I do all I can to honor my appointments." This is a dig against any other contractors they might be considering. When a prospect calls three contractors, at least one of them does not show up at all or is more than an hour late and never calls to say he will be late. Remodelers have a reputation of being unreliable. When they are late, they help validate that reputation.

Be sure to introduce yourself to everyone you encounter during your visit. Prospects are impressed when you shake hands with their children. With remodeling projects that will last for weeks or months, it's important for the parents to know the children will feel comfortable with you. Jot down their names so you will be able to greet them personally at your next meeting.

When I go on calls, my objective is to make a sale. If I get there and find one of the decision makers was unable to make the appointment, I immediately label this approach as unsuccessful. I am not going to continue on a closing path unless something happens to change that assessment. I'm not going to walk out, of course, but I change from a selling mode to making a favorable impression for our next appointment. I will explore the project with the prospect who is there and plan on closing during the next visit.

If you show up on time, your attire is neat and clean, and the decision makers are there, your approach has been successful. You may think this is petty stuff, but I disagree. We are not talking about building additions. We are talking about building value, showing ourselves worthy of the price we charge for our work. Have some of you ever wondered why prospects would pay another company as much as twice the price you charged? The answer starts in the approach.

2. **Warm-up:** *Your goal in the warm-up is to get the prospects to like you and to trust you.*

If I had to pick one segment of the sales process as the most important, it would be the warm-up. People don't like buying from people they don't like or trust. This doesn't mean you have to befriend your prospects before you can sell them anything, but it does mean they want to have a good feeling about you before they agree to entrust you with their confidence, home, and money.

How can we do all that in a matter of a few minutes? Spend a little time talking with your prospects about anything other than the project. For some of you, this will be hard at first, but it will soon become your favorite part of the selling process. After you have finished your approach, go right into some small talk. Time yourself, and don't discuss the project for at least five minutes. My first questions are, "How long have you folks lived in this house? Is this your first home together? Where are you originally from? Have you lived here all your life?" (A wise old man responded, "Not yet.") "I see you have a recreational vehicle out front, are you able to use it much? Where is your favorite camping spot?"

Find something to talk about. You will know you are on the right subject when the folks start rambling on without any prompting from you. This is the first indication that they feel at ease with you. Most of us like to talk about ourselves, but we get little opportunity to do so. Give your prospects that opportunity. They will like you instantly.

To enjoy the kind of sales success the remodeling business affords, you have to like people. If you don't and are interested only in selling a job, that will become obvious during the warm-up. The prospects will get a cold feeling about you, not the warmth they are seeking in a relationship.

Practice the warm-up at every opportunity. You will be excited to see how much joy a person gets in talking about himself. Prospects will share a lot of information with you, much of which you have no need to know. What you want to know before you leave the warm-up:

- How long have the folks been considering the project? (You want to know this so you can use it in the close when they say they want to think about it.)
- Is this a job you want? (Can you make money on this project?)
- Do you think you can satisfy these prospects? (Have they talked of only bad experiences? If so, that's a sign that nobody can satisfy them.)

Good salespeople don't have trouble selling jobs. They have to be careful not to oversell. By overselling, I mean bringing in jobs that don't fit the company or that involve a prospect who will be more trouble than the job is worth. Once you have a "bad" customer, you will give all you own to get rid of them. I had one who looked bad even in the warm-up, but my sales ego got in the way and I sold the job anyway. Talk with contractors about their worst jobs and they all will say they saw the danger signs in the warm-up. The warm-up is indeed the segment of the sell where the prospect will tell you how to sell them. Be an attentive listener. I often go on sales calls to observe other salespeople, and I hear many points the salespeople don't. They are so busy worrying about what they are going to say next that they don't listen.

If you knew that in the warm-up the prospects will tell you how to sell them, would you listen better? Well, they will every time. Of course, they aren't going to say, "Here's how to sell me." They will say, "We don't like to be pressured." Or "We like to shop around before we buy." Or "We're not going to make a decision today." Or "We are just gathering information now, we won't have the money for several more months." You have heard these before, I'm sure. You probably viewed them as negative indicators. You are going to learn how to turn those objections into positives for you and your prospect in the close.

In a successful warm-up, you talk about events other than the project. You become acquainted with the prospects in a personal way. You learn something about the children, and you include them in the conversation if they are present. You learn how long the prospects have been thinking about the project. They tell you how to sell them, although they may express it in a negative manner. You determine if these prospects and this job are well suited to your company. You can tell that these people like you.

3. **Qualifying:** *The goal of qualifying is to determine how much money the prospects want to spend, how much they can spend, and where the money is coming from.*

This segment of the Full Routine can save you a lot of time. It's a big mistake to assume that every prospect has the ability to pay for the project. At the end of the warm-up, I start talking about the type of work the prospects had in mind. Now, I want to know what kind of money they plan to invest. I don't think for a second that they have no idea what the project will cost. They might be wrong, but they have an idea.

I assume all prospects are payment buyers. Even if they are borrowing from the bank and not using my financial sources, they are going to make payments to somebody. That means they need to know how much the job will cost in monthly payments. When you throw out a number like $25,000 to payment buyers, you might as well be talking a foreign language. They don't know whether they can afford it or not until they know the monthly payment.

As I mentioned earlier, you should offer financing to your clients. There are many benefits. The prospects are not as concerned about the total price. They don't run off to their own bank, only to hear the banker say, "Before you do anything, why don't you get an estimate from my neighbor?" We finance about 20 percent of our sales through lending institutions with which we have dealer agreements. These agreements allow me to act on behalf of the institutions. I am able to take the credit application and process all the loan papers without the customer leaving the house.

Get an agreement with a lender. This is perhaps the biggest difference between making a living and making money. I have sold many jobs by saying, "Mr. and Mrs. Prospect, for just another $45 a month I can replace all the windows. It's already costing you more than that not to have them."

When you ask the prospects the money question, you will see if your warm-up was successful. If they don't trust you, they will not give the information freely. Many contractors find it very difficult to find out the prospect's budget. Once you start doing warm-ups, it will become much easier. I say, "Mr. and Mrs. Prospect, as I'm sure you are aware, kitchens vary greatly in price. We had a client a few months back who chose cabinetry worth more than $30,000, and we recently did a kitchen with $5,000 cabinets. I need some guidance from you so I can recommend products that will be within the price you want to pay. In terms of a monthly payment, how much did you plan to invest in this project?" If they say, "We don't have any idea," or "We called you to see how much it would cost," try again. "What I'm saying is that we can build and design your kitchen according to your desires and your budget. We're very good at it, too. But I need to know what dollar amount you want me to work with." If this doesn't work, start throwing out money numbers until they grab one: $200-$300 a month, $300-$400, and so on.

If they tell me they will be paying cash, I ask if they will be taking out a home-equity loan. I want to know this because home equity determines the budget for many homeowners. If I design a $50,000 job and they only have $20,000 of borrowing power, I will have created another nice drawing for the file. If they have obtained the money already or are paying out of their personal resources, they certainly will know their budget. Whatever their circumstances, you must find out what your prospects can spend.

Once you have determined that amount, you can show products and designs to fit it. I realize that what people want to pay and what they will actually pay are two different things. When they give me a number, I tell them whether or not their number is realistic. If it is, I'm ready to present. If it is not, we continue discussing the money.

In qualifying, I'm often able to sense if additional sales calls will be required. There is rarely a need for more than one sales call on roofing, siding, windows, and other specialty projects. Larger projects require more selling. Before I leave the first call on a large project, I give a ballpark price and a trial close (covered in the section on closes). Whatever the project, don't make your job so hard that you don't see the easy sale. Some people are ready to buy, so be ready to sell. I read about a survey showing that 8 percent of new homebuyers purchased a home on the first visit. If that's true, how many remodeling jobs should you be closing on the first visit?

4. **Presentation**: *The goal of the presentation is to convince the prospects that your products and your company are what they need.*

There are two distinctly different presentations that need to be made, the first on your products and the second on your company. Once the scope of the project has been determined and you are prepared to suggest products and make recommendations, your presentation is under way.

Most people are visual. They want to see something, not just hear your pitch. Don't disappoint them. You should have samples and pictures. When showing products for different areas of the job, be prepared to give a choice of at least two. This allows the prospects to feel that they are making the decision and that you aren't pushing a line of products just so you can win an incentive trip. It's also good for prospects to have the opportunity to give me some "noes" before we get into the close. When they say "no" to one product, they are saying "yes" to another.

Know your products because: "Knowledge instills confidence, confidence instills enthusiasm, and enthusiasm sells." Be careful not to confuse your prospects with information. They are interested only in the product features that will directly benefit them. Normally, people buy when they perceive the value to exceed the price. Keep that in mind as you give your presentation.

Selling is the transference of feeling. If you are sold on your products, this will show (the reverse is also true). Most sales decisions boil down to price or product, so be sure to take care of the product. Don't move on until the prospects have picked out the products and the colors. Every time they go through the exercise selection, they are buying mentally. Ask after all the products have been selected, "Mr. and Mrs. Prospect, is there any question as to whether the products you have selected will meet your needs?" A "no" response means you are ready to present your company. Say, "It is very important that you select quality products. You have been wise in that selection. It is even more important that the company you select can properly install those products. Let me tell you why I feel it is important for you to select our company."

This is when the company presentation book comes out. If you don't have a presentation book, get one. The book should include licenses, insurance certificates, letters of recommendation from previous customers, newspaper or magazine articles about your company, and photos showing your work. I tell my prospects that, unfortunately, many people tend to think of all remodelers as equal. Then I show pictures I have taken of bad jobs or horror stories clipped from the newspaper. I think we owe it to our prospects to educate them about bad contractors. I do not believe in name-calling, but to say, "You get what you pay for" is not enough. In certain instances, actually take your prospects for a drive to show them botched jobs, and then show them some of your jobs. Make certain your prospects are aware that they have a choice — either choose you (and get a good job) or choose someone else (and take their chances).

Then, after you have finished the presentation of your company, ask, "Do you have any concerns as to whether our company can give you the type of quality you are looking for? Mr. and Mrs. Prospect, let me ask you one question. Assuming for just a moment that price is not a factor, if the project we discussed is affordable, would you do business with our company?" If they say "yes," then you know the only thing to keep them from buying would be price. If they say "no," then price is not the sticking point and there's no need to discuss it. You have missed the boat somewhere. You need to backtrack and get a "yes" answer before you close.

5. Close: *The goal of the close is to leave with a contract.*

The close is just that. It's the end. All other segments of the sale must have been executed successfully or you won't be successful in the close. The close is where all of your mistakes manifest themselves or your good works will pay off. Don't try to close until you are ready and the time is right. Many salespeople think they are not good closers when they don't get the job. Chances are those people are not good approachers, warm-uppers, qualifiers, or presenters. Get good at those, and the close becomes much easier.

It's only natural to experience a little anxiety when you start closing. You are about to find out if your efforts will be rewarded. Some prospects will close themselves by saying, "That sounds great to me. When can you start?" or "Let's do it." I don't have to tell you that these are not the typical responses. Human nature is to put off decisions that don't have to be made. The remodeling salesperson often must be able to show convincingly that improving is better than moving, that the project is not an overkill for the neighborhood, that the investment in the property is sound, that today is a better day to buy than tomorrow, that doing business with you is better than doing business with someone else. The list could go on and on. But knowing that is half the battle.

To close, you must be in a closing situation — the decision makers are present, the ability to buy has been established, and the products have been selected.

Let's take a look at the close. First, go back over the work that you propose to do in as much detail as you can. This is your last attempt to build value. Since value needs to exceed price for a sale to take place, you know you have done a good job when the prospects say, "That sounds like a good deal to me." If you hear an objection, don't be unprepared. Anyone who's been selling remodeling for a month probably has heard nearly all of the objections there are. It's time you started anticipating these objections.

The objection I used to hear quite often is, "That's too much money." I try to eliminate it before it comes up. I say, "Mr. and Mrs. Prospect, before I give you the price of your project, let me tell you, it costs too much. When was the last time you or I bought something that didn't cost too much? Everything costs too much. I wish I could make this job cost less, but I can't. I can only say that, based on my previous buying experiences, your job is never going to cost less than it does today. Now, there are two attitudes you can take when I give you the price. One is, 'Let's see how we can afford to do the project.' The other is, 'Let's see how we can't afford it.' Can we all agree on at least trying to have the 'let's see how we can afford it' attitude?" That little speech makes them come up with another reason other than "too much." It also elevates their thinking. If they were figuring this is going to cost $5,000, they may now be estimating $6,000.

Once you give the price, don't say a word. You are done talking! There are countless ways to close, several of which are described below. Deciding which close to use depends on many factors, but I almost always use the payment close.

- **The Payment Close:** With this close, the salesperson states the price as a monthly payment. Even though the prospects may be cash buyers, give them the option of changing their mind. The payment amount is much softer than the total price. "Mr. and Mrs. Prospect, we can do all the work we talked about for $113.66 a month on a no penalty for early payout, tax-deductible loan. That's a total price of $9,936.24." Normally, they have to ask again about the total price, because they don't hear it, they are so taken with how affordable the monthly payments are.

- **The Trial Close:** Trial closes are often used prior to the "big" close. This is one of those closes where I look for the chance to use it as early and as often as possible. I might say, "When would you want us to schedule this project?" I want to hear, "When could you schedule it?" Or I might say, "I noticed you had some bricks missing from your front stoop. While our mason is here, would you like for me to fix that? There would be no charge." How they respond to these questions lets me know exactly where I stand.

- **The Odd-Cents Close:** Never give a price in nice round numbers like $10,000. Give $9,936.24. You cut off $64, but it sounds like a thousand less. When you give cents, you convey to your prospects that you have figured this job to the penny and not just rounded it off to the next hundred or thousand.

- **The Assumptive Close:** You have given the price and you wait for no opposition and encourage none. Don't say, "Well, what do you think?" or "Do you want us to do the work?"

Just pull out your contract (or credit application first if they are financing) and move into the secondary close.

- **The Secondary Close:** Documents in hand, say, "Mr. Prospect, what is your full name?" If he gives you his name, you are closing the deal. If he doesn't, you'd better be ready for the tennis-racket close.

- **The "Tennis-Racket" Close:** In the close, you should talk only when absolutely necessary. That means you should not answer any questions that can be answered by the prospects. It sometimes requires volleying questions and answers with them. The first question I hear when I ask for the full name is, "Does this mean we are buying?" My response is, "Yes, it does." "Well, we need to think this over." "Just what do you need to think over, Mr. Prospect?" "We haven't talked with anyone but you. We need to get other estimates." "Why is that, Mrs. Prospect?" Recognize these for what they are. They are stalls. If you accept these stalls, you will lose more than 90 percent of your sales. Rarely do prospects think it over and call you back. At the most, half will shop around. A stall is not your enemy. People always have two reasons for not buying — the reason that sounds good and the real reason. "Look around" and "think about it" are "sounds good" reasons. That is what they are supposed to say and what salespeople are used to hearing. You must get to the real reason. The tennis-racket close, in which you hit the question back to the prospects, forces them to justify their reasons, often talking themselves into buying without any further comments from you. Remember, there also are two reasons why people don't buy — product and price. If they told you at the end of the presentation that, without considering the price, they would like to have your product, a stall may indicate the price needs to be justified. I didn't say, "Drop the price." It's way too early to consider that. But it does bring up the next closing technique.

- **The "Give Me Your Best Price" Close:** This is for the prospects who rarely allow you to complete a sentence without interrupting with, "All I want is your best price." As a salesperson you should ask yourself, "What are they going to do with my best price?" The answer is that they'll use it to shop around. Don't play that game. Instead, ask the prospects what constitutes best price. Is best price the lowest price? After that has been established, ask if they are in a position to recognize a best price. If the response to that is "yes," I ask this: "If I were to give you the very best price I could possibly give, would you give me a 'yes' or 'no'?" This puts the burden right back on them. I have given the prospects enough information to make a decision. If the decision is "no," I'll deal with it. But I hate to leave without a decision.

- **The Sense-Of-Urgency Close:** Remember to ask yourself three questions before you go into the appointment: (1) Why should they buy my product? (2) Why should they buy them from me? (3) Why should they buy them today? We are all procrastinators. If we feel like we can get the same thing tomorrow without making a decision today, why should we make a decision today? We buy a car because it might not be there tomorrow, especially a used car. We buy a house because someone else may buy it. Why should someone buy your siding today? Could it be interest rates are getting ready to go up? (Regardless of whether the customer is financing the project or not, interest rates do affect the cost of goods.) Do you have a job that has been put on hold due to permit hold-ups and your best crew can get in on their job immediately? You need to have an honest story of why today is a better day to buy your products than tomorrow. This close is like all closes, use it when you need it.

- **The "Getting Other Estimates" Close:** When the prospect says, "We need to get other estimates." You say, "How many estimates did you want? That's fine. I can provide you with at least that many." Not exactly the answer they were looking for, but we are manufacturers, right? We can build the project a number of different ways. Apologize for perhaps playing too much mind reader and putting too much of your twist on the project and not enough of theirs. "Let's take a few minutes and view the project from another angle." Another way to handle the "getting other estimates" close is to say something like, "Mr. and Mrs. Jones, let me interject some comments that might save you a great deal of time in your shopping endeavor. Surveys have shown that most people buy when they find something they like. So, with that in mind, I'm concerned that I didn't show you what you were looking for, would that statement be true?" If they say "yes," then find out where you missed. If they say "no," then ask, "Why would you need to get another estimate? You two aren't professional shoppers, are you? I was just wondering. I've seen on TV where companies send customers out to shop the competition." (My personality and level of confidence allow me to say these kinds of things, although they may appear very awkward for you.) "Mr. and Mrs. Jones, what are you looking for? Lowest price, good quality, or good service? Bear in mind, you can only get two of the three. If you want the last two, I'm your company. If you want lowest price, I hate to say this, but you will probably be calling me later. Would you rather pay a little bit more than you expected to spend and get the results you wanted or would you rather end up paying a lot more by paying twice? Most home improvements are done because someone didn't do the job right the first time. Let's do business together to ensure that doesn't happen to you!"

- **The "You Deserve It" Close:** Many people never get what they really want because they don't think they deserve it. My parents worked extremely hard to raise a family, they were both products of the Great Depression. Many of your prospects may be spending more on their remodeling than they paid for their homes. They may have raised five children in the house and, now that all the children are gone, they are considering expanding. They often question their sanity. A good salesperson is also a good therapist. "Mr. and Mrs. Jones, I have many customers who go through the same thought process you are going through. Chances are, you couldn't afford to do this type of project while you were paying for braces on teeth, schools, etc. You don't have that now. You've been in the neighborhood a long time. You are obviously very settled and comfortable here. You just have some plans to make the house more enjoyable and that's wonderful. And you know what else, Mr. and Mrs. Jones? You deserve it. Anybody who can raise five children deserves a reward. Congratulations!"

- **The "Third No" Close:** My first sales manager taught me to ignore "no" until I had heard it at least three times. Unless they show it with body language (such as standing up for you to leave), often a "no" from prospects means "not now, keep selling." I heard that 80 percent of all sales are made after the fifth closing attempt (that doesn't mean five visits), and only 10 percent of all salespeople have the ability to ask for the sale more than five times. That explains why some salespeople are rich. It also explains why sometimes it appears that you did all the work and another company ends up getting the job. You were probably just one "no" away. It is natural for prospects to offer resistance. I do when I'm the buyer because I want to see if the person trying to sell me is sold himself or just trying to make some money off me. There are certainly times when a "no" should be taken as a "no" without further questions, but the sales process is rarely one of those times unless you are using the negative-sales close.

- **The Negative-Sales Close:** I'm sure you have discovered this close. You just have to learn to use it to your advantage. People often want what they can't have. When they sense you rejecting them (when you say such things as, "If I could do this job, I don't know when it would be," or "We normally don't do these type projects," or "I'm not sure we could get the financing arranged"), they seem to take on the selling role themselves. When you take the attitude, "I don't care if I get this job or not," you often get it. Your prospects stop thinking that you are concerned about your personal gain. This is one reason a salesperson is able to sell a job immediately after selling another big job. Be aware of that fact and go on every lead you can after you sell a nice job, rather than sitting back counting your money.

- **The "Ben Franklin" Close**: Many people have a difficult time making decisions. That's when I use one of my favorites — the "Ben Franklin" close. It's said that Franklin used this approach personally, and I have found it most useful in my personal life. It removes the emotion from the decision-making process. Get out a piece of paper and draw a line down the middle and say, "Mr. and Mrs. Prospect, making a big decision is often difficult. Let's try to remove the emotion and make a logical decision based on facts. This was a method used by Ben Franklin, not a bad guy to copy. Let's look at the reasons to put siding on the house." Let the prospects spend some time doing this. Help them only if they get bogged down. After they have listed six or more reasons, go over to the other column and have them list the reasons not to buy. I cannot remember anyone ever having more than two. You can say, "We have six reasons to buy, and one reason not to buy. The decision is clear, wouldn't you say?" You can also deal with the negative reasons and find out why they are negative. They don't get any better than this close.

- **The "Porch Light" Close:** One of the most common objections is, "We want to think about it." No problem. That calls for the "porch light" close. Ask the prospects what they want to think about and remind them that they told you (in the warm-up) how long they have been thinking about this project. Then say, "You told me you had been thinking about siding since you painted your house seven years ago. Don't you agree it's time to stop thinking and start doing?" If every effort fails and the prospects insist they need to discuss the job privately, get up without hesitation and start gathering your possessions.

Offer one of these options: (1) "I have some paper work I need to take care of. Take your time, talk it over, and just flick the porch light when you have made a decision," (2) "I have to run down the road and check on another project, I'll stop by in about thirty minutes," or (3) "I haven't had lunch, I'm going to go eat. I'll check back by in a half-hour or so." Don't ask if that's okay. They will tell you if it is or isn't. Sell to your prospects the way your children sell to you. This close is a humdinger. Leave something in the house when you go out, such as a product sample, that assures you will get back in. If you get a "no," at least you will get it to your face and you have one more opportunity to deal with it.

- **The "Just Do It" Close:** Selling takes fortitude. Most people are followers. They want and need to be told what to do. I have sold many a job by telling the prospects, "Just do it."

- **The "If I Could, Would You?" Close:** This is a great closing technique, with the same rationale as the tennis-racket close. The prospects ask, "Can you cut the price to $5,000 instead of $10,000?" Your response should be, "Mr. and Mrs. Prospect, if I could, would you give me your business?" If they answer "yes," then we deal with the price. If they ask, "Could you have our project completed by Christmas?" you respond, "If I could, would you give me your business?"

- **The "Just Get Their Signature" Close:** Many salespeople employ this technique. I hate it and strongly encourage you to adopt other methods. Those who use this technique believe that, if you throw enough stuff against the wall, some of it is bound to stick. They say, "Go ahead and sign and, if you decide to cancel, just return the form." When I walk out of a house, I want to know that I have a firm deal and won't have to worry about cancellations. When prospects ask me if they have the right to cancel, I say, "Yes. If that's a consideration, however, please don't sign the contract." If there is an objection that needs to be handled, I want to deal with it now. Just bringing in contracts gives everyone a false sense of security. You have almost gone the distance. Hang in there for one more objection and make a firm sale.

- **The "What Do I Have to Do?" Close:** I use this one as much as any other. "Mr. and Mrs. Prospect, we share something in common. I have siding and you need siding. Tell me what I need to do for us to get together." If they say, "Nothing," I say, "Now I can't do it for nothing, but that's a start. Short of nothing, what can I do?" Stay on it until you find out what the prospect wants. Maybe it's a $10,000 job for $5,000. No sale, of course, but at least you will leave knowing what the problem was.

- **The Apology Close**: When all else fails, try this close. You must be very sincere when using it. As you are on the way out, turn and say, "Mr. and Mrs. Prospect, I apologize for being such an inept salesperson. I honestly believe that I have the product and service that are best suited for you. How could I have better conveyed that message to you?" The prospects may give you the information you need to make the sale. When used properly, this close can be most effective.

No close works all the time and some closes work better than others, depending on the situation. It's important to be able to employ many different techniques. Rarely will you use only one. I will use the payment close, odd-cents close, secondary close, assumptive close, tennis-racket close, "If I could, would you?" close, and the "third no" close on almost every sales call I make. Practice them all, and find the closes with which you are most comfortable. Keep in mind that the hardest closes are often the most effective. The truth is, they sound harder than they actually are.

A good opportunity to try out a new technique is when you have prospects who you just know aren't going to buy from you. Since you have nothing to lose, try something new, practice on them. Don't be shocked when they buy.

While closing is only one part of the Full Routine, it's definitely the report card by which all sales people are ultimately measured. If you are doing the other parts well, you will close well. It's your final exam. You must study and be prepared. After you finish with the close and don't get the job, take inventory of yourself before you drive off. Ask what you did right and what you did wrong. Make sure you gave them the opportunity to buy. That means asking them to. Did you do all that you could? If you did, do the same thing on the next call. With one appointment a day, you are doing well to sell one job a week. With two appointments a day you should sell three jobs a week.

6. **Follow-up:** *Your goal in the follow-up is to create a customer for life.*

This is the last segment of the selling process. I view it as the last two-tenths of a marathon. A marathon run is 26.2 miles. Getting to the close is like getting to the 26-mile marker. But the last two-tenths of a mile still have to be run. The follow-up is easy, so easy it tends to be neglected. It begins when the customers sign the contract. I shake both of their hands and congratulate them on what I consider to be a wise investment. I also thank them for the trust and confidence they have placed in my company and tell them I will not do anything to betray that trust and confidence. My unspoken message is: "Don't betray me either by canceling."

I got two or three cancellations a year. That's not many, but it's two or three more than I wanted. Every customer suffers "buyer's remorse," when the purchasers question if they've made the right decision. Buyers will sometimes go to someone else for reassurance and that person will often determine the fate of the decision. For example, I always talk to my wife. Her response always is, "You get buyer's remorse about everything." She walks off, and that's the end of the conversation. My remorse is cured. If I went to a neighbor who said, "I can't believe you didn't get three estimates. Are you still within your three-day cancellation period?" I might very well change my mind.

After you sell a job, you want to make certain that you're the person your clients consult. Get in touch with them within twenty-four hours after you have made the sale. Some companies send a letter thanking them for their business. That could reach them too late. Other companies send a floral arrangement. What you do is up to you. Just be sure you are sensitive to buyer's remorse and have something in place to combat it.

Buyer's remorse doesn't often occur with large jobs (jobs which probably involve more than one sales call). Still, the more time you have invested in selling the job, the more a cancellation hurts.

Follow-up also means going to your job site. Many companies turn the production responsibility over to someone else after the sale, but you should still show your face. The customers made the deal with you. They feel better seeing you on the job. This is when you might ask your customers for names of friends, relatives, and neighbors to whom you can show your products. Tell them you realize that these people may not be in the market now, but you would like to show them what you offer in hopes that you can be of service to them in the future.

Make sure your job sign is properly displayed while your crews are working. In just one year, our company had 145 calls off job signs. A salesperson can make a good living from those leads.

After the job is completed, send a thank-you card at minimum. I sent a nice potted plant. Then, I sent a survey sheet asking the clients to rate us in about ten different categories varying from how they were treated on the phone to whether we could use them as a reference.

After the initial follow-up has been completed, I encourage contact throughout the year. My company mailed out holiday cards. There are numerous ways you can do this follow-up. Just be sure you do it. When a customer calls you back the second time, the sale is much easier. You should sell 80 percent of your referrals and 90 percent of your previous customers.

That last little "two-tenths of a mile" of a sales call can be very profitable.

Chapter 31

WHY DO YOU THINK PEOPLE CALL YOU? THEY WANT TO BE SOLD!

In the remodeling business, we often hear our prospects say, "We don't know if we should move or improve." Guess what? Unless you are also a real-estate agent, they are actually saying, "Sell us on why we should improve." If they had wanted to move, the Realtor would be there and not you.

A major philosophical difference between many remodeling salespeople and me is that I firmly believe people want to be sold. They don't want to keep shopping. They want to be sold on doing business with you so they can go on to something else. Don't make it hard on your prospects to buy.

I had two houses I wanted to sell. One was located in a beach-resort area. I knew by watching and observing the area who the top real-estate agents in that community were. I called one, and she did not let me down. She was everything I had thought she would be. She looked at the house, called me, told me how much she thought she could sell the house for, and faxed me a listing contract to sign. In forty-five days, she called to tell me she had an offer on the house, which I accepted. I had figured it would take two full seasons to sell the house. I didn't think anybody would buy beach property in the winter. She proved me wrong. I never met this Realtor until I went down to do my walk-through. I chose her based on the number of "sold" signs I had seen over the years with her name on them. When I called her, my job was hers to lose, not hers to get.

About that same time, I also put my personal house on the market for sale. Again, I picked the Realtor I thought was the best in our area. When he came out to my house, he suggested that I call two of the other top Realtors in the area and get their opinions.

I was shocked! He had given me absolutely no reason why I should not sign a listing agreement with him. Eventually, I did list my house with him, but only because of errors made by another Realtor. If that second Realtor had not made the errors, he would have gotten my listing. You will get sales because someone else messed up, but don't count on making a living that way. Make a living by selling your services and not by recommending the services of your competitors!

I want to share another story with you. My wife wanted a new car. The car she wanted was a new offering for that year, and none of the dealers in our immediate area had one. I found a dealer in a nearby city who had several. My wife and I drove the distance to check out the car. After taking it for a test drive, she drove it back to the dealership. The salesperson asked how she had liked it, and she told him she loved it. He said, "Let me get you a brochure on it." Brochure! Was he nuts? How about getting some plates to put on the car so we could drive it home? Your instant response might be, "What a dummy." How many times might your techniques have fit the same modus operandi of that dummy? More times than you care to realize, you have inadvertently sent a prospect to the telephone to call another contractor when they had planned for you to be the only call they made.

People want to be sold. Help them out by doing just that!

Chapter 32

DON'T PAY THE PRICE WITHOUT ENJOYING THE SUCCESS

Although this book is about how to make money, always remember there is much more to life than making money. My dad always said, "You've got problems with money, and you've got problems without money, I'll take the problems with money." Whenever I hear someone say, "Money will not make you happy," I do my best to size them up to see if they were speaking from experience. I always figured it was a broke person saying that in an effort to make themselves feel better. But it is true that money will not make you happy. Look around you. For the most part, the people with money are working themselves to death in an effort to obtain more.

USA TODAY did an article on millionaires. They asked millionaires how much money would be enough. The overall response was, "If I had twice what I have, I would be comfortable." These were millionaires talking! We should all learn from this. There is no such thing as enough money. You will never have enough money if money is your benchmark for happiness. Money should be a way for you to keep score. In a sports contest, the team with the most points wins. When the game is over, the game is over. Our work is a game as well, don't take it too seriously. Have some fun. In the overall scheme of things, how important is a room addition, a new kitchen, or a bathroom renovation? Each day, play the game for the amount of hours you choose. When the buzzer sounds, go play another game. Start the remodeling game again the next day. Remember that there are things that need your attention more than your business. Find out what they are and devote time to them.

As I mentioned, my father was a government employee. His vocation never paid him much money. When he retired his salary was $21,000 a year. His hobby, however, was making money. Every extra cent went into investments. He spent a great deal of time recording the progress of each of these investments. I used to think the greatest thrill he got each day was going to the mailbox hoping to find a dividend check or a statement on one of his accounts.

Dad was diagnosed with cancer at the age of 69. He was told he had maybe a year or two to live. Still, his attitude on life was as pleasant as ever. Toward the end, his health deteriorated rapidly before my eyes. I realized just how bad he must have been feeling when I visited him one Saturday and all his unopened mail just sat by his chair. I asked if he would like for me to open his mail. He said, "No, I want you to take me outside so I can look at the grapevines and the fig bushes." Sensing that the precious time with my father was very short, I asked him, "Dad, if you had to do it all over again, what would you do differently?" He said, "I would spend more time with you kids. Of all those meetings I attended, only a few of them amounted to anything." My dad died in 1993 at the age of 71. He missed the bullish stock market of the 1990s. Even so, he died a multimillionaire.

I had known for a long time that I needed to prepare myself for this game called work. I was always told, "Life is a long row to hoe," "No pain, no gain," and "There is a high price to be paid for success." We all need to be careful about what games we engage in. Some of them take much more out of us than we ever wanted to give. Often, we are not even aware of how much we are giving. How tragic it would be for us to come to our end and realize we had paid the price for success without enjoying the success itself.

Becoming a millionaire and becoming rich are often not the same thing. You can be rich without money. However, if becoming a millionaire is one of your goals, you are in a business that will produce many. Will you be one?

HAPPY SELLING!!!

OTHER PRODUCTS BY PHIL REA

Through his company, Phil Rea & Associates, the author offers a range of business improvement products including:

1. ***Business Consultant:*** This includes evaluations with businesses committed to improving their operation and their bottom line. Everything from goal planning with key employees to visiting job sites. Followed by a comprehensive report detailing Phil's findings and recommendations. His consulting services have offered creative approaches to improving a number of remodeling businesses.

2. ***Sales Trainer:*** Phil has conducted more one-on-one sales training with remodeling salespeople than any other sales trainer in recent years. He does it all, from door-to-door prospecting to closing sales.

3. ***Comprehensive half-day and full-day seminars***: Phil has brought his message to a wide range of audiences and settings...from national corporate sales meetings and international conventions to in-house training seminars.

4. ***Audio tapes:*** A comprehensive set of audio tapes directed exclusively to the remodeling salesperson. These tapes cover Phil's sales and marketing process in great detail:

    - ***"How To Sell Remodeling" (two-tape set)***
      This widely acclaimed presentation is a must-hear for the building industry salesperson. Phil's unique FULL ROUTINE approach will put money in any salesperson's pocket...***quickly!***

    - ***"Salesperson or Order Taker...What's It Going To Be?"***
      Everybody is in the selling business, but few are SALESPEOPLE...learn what a difference it can make.

- ***"Hate Competition? Me, Too! How To Get Folks To Call You...Any Only You!"***
  In this time of increased competition, Phil Rea lets you know how to not only GET customers, but how to get them to call you ... and only you.

- ***"Sell Financing And Sell More Jobs"***
  People may be paying you cash, but most are making payments to somebody. When you start selling payments, your sales will soar.

For more information, contact:

Phil Rea & Associates, P.O. Box 1188, Newport News, VA 23601
Call Toll Free: 800-441-7445 Fax: (757) 596-3325
E-mail: philrea@aol.com